INCREASE YOUR WORD POWER

KEY

Woxbrandt / Kunze

BEAVER BOOKS

© **Beaver Books**   Dr. C. Kunze / B. Woxbrandt

Alle Rechte vorbehalten

All rights reserved. No part of this publication may be reproduced or utilized, in any forms or by any means, without the prior permission of the copyright holders and publishers.

Die Deutsche Bibliothek - CIP-Einheitsaufnahme

Woxbrandt, Barbro:
Increase your wordpower / Woxbrandt / Kunze. - Frankfurt am Main : Beaver Books

Key. - 1997
    ISBN 3 - 926686 - 25 - 1

BEAVER BOOKS, Marburger Str. 15, 60487 Frankfurt/Main
Tel. 069/774047 • Fax 069/704635

INCREASE YOUR WORDPOWER • KEY

INCREASE YOUR WORDPOWER 1 • Key	5
Animal Kingdom	5
Born to be Wild	5
Back on the Farm	5
Cluster Club	5
Wordpower Rockets	6
Over the Moon	7
Cool Collocations	7
Euro Quiz	7
Time for a Rhyme	8
Rhyme Groups	8
Too many Cooks Spoil the Broth!	8
Part & Parcel	8
How British are you?	9
Compose a Compound	9
Synonyms / Synonym Quartets	9
Mixed Bag Quiz	10
Link and Learn	10
Sort out the Sport	11
Ups and Downs / Pair them Up!	11
Homophones	11
Odd One Out!	12
Super Similes / More Similes	12
Antonyms	12
Opposites	13
What's Up?	13
In a Class of its Own	13
Shared Beginnings	13
Landmarks	14
Straight from the Horse's Mouth / Animal Idioms	14
Look in the right Place	14
Falling into Place	14
Don't count your Chickens . . .	15
Look for Links	15
Fill that Gap	15
Vexing Vowels	16
It's how you say it	16
Scrabble	17
Be as Good as your Word	17
Dial a Word	18
Famous Last Words	18
INCREASE YOUR WORDPOWER 2 • Key	21
Tips for Teachers	47

Animal Kingdom 5

ANIMAL	YOUNG	FEMALE	MALE
cow	calf	cow	bull
duck	duckling	duck	drake
horse	foal	mare	stallion
goose	gosling	goose	gander
pig	piglet	sow	boar
cat	kitten	—	tom
sheep	lamb	ewe	ram
chicken	chicken	hen	cock
dog	puppy	bitch	—

Born to be Wild 6

Lions **roar**   Elephants **trumpet**
Birds **sing**   Wolves **howl**
Snakes **hiss**   Monkeys **chatter**

Many elephants make **a herd**
Many lions make **a pride**
Many wolves make **a pack**
Many bees make **a swarm**
Many sheep make **a flock**
Many hens make **a brood**

Back on the Farm 7

Match the animals with the sounds.

Sheep **bleat**   Cocks **crow**
Ducks **quack**   Hens **cackle**
Cows **moo**   Geese **honk**
Pigs **grunt**   Owls **hoot**
Horses **neigh**   Bees **hum**
Cats **miaow**   Frogs **croak**
Dogs **bark**

Which animals have

paws: cats, dogs, tigers, lions, wolves
fur: cats, dogs, tigers, lions, wolves, monkeys
wings: ducks, cocks, hens, geese, eagles, owls, bees
tails: all of the animals except the frogs and bees
hooves: horses, cows, sheep
horns: cows
beaks: ducks, geese, hens, eagles, owls, cocks

Cluster Club 8

— ea —

4 Letters

bead bear beat dead dear east fear
feat gear head heal heap hear lead
leap meal mean near pear read real
reap sear tear veal zeal

5 Letters

beach beard beast bleak bread break cheap
cheat clear creak death early earth feast
heard heart learn lease peace pearl plead
reach react spear steal teach treat yeast

6 Letters

appeal appear breast breath health meagre
nearly reason please preach season wealth

7 Letters and more

appease feather heather leather meander
meaning measles measure stealth teacher
treacle treason weather nearest meaning
pleasure treasure clearing breakfast preacher

— ou —

4 Letters

soul foul four loud noun bout lout

5 Letters

about around cloud couch cough count
court doubt dough found gouge house
louse mould mount mourn mouse mouth
pouch pound round sound south touch

6 Letters

arouse   blouse   bounty   couple
course   double   ground   lounge
plough   should   though   trough

7 Letters and more

boulder   carouse   carousel   country
courage   foundry   gourmet   moulder
nervous   trouble   boundary   courtesy
fountain generous mountain   neighbour
scrounge shoulder smoulder   foundation
malicious generous dangerous

—— oa ——

4 Letters

boar	boat	coal	coat	coax
foal	foam	goad	goal	goat
hoax	load	loaf	loan	moan
moat	road	roam	roar	soap
soar	toad			

5 Letters

board	boast	coach	coast	gloat
hoard	hoary	poach	roach	roast
stoat	toast			

6 Letters and more

hoarse   coarse   loathe   coalition   coagulate

Wordpower Rockets

Here are some examples of possible words

3 Letters

art	eat	ham	hat	mad	mat
rat	sad	sat	set	tar	tea

4 Letters

dame	dare	dash	date	dead	deed
deem	ease	east	head	heat	made
mash	mast	mate	mead	meat	mere
rash	rate	read	ream	rest	same
seam	seed	sham	shed	star	stem
tame	team	tear	teem	test	tree

5 Letters

asset	death	drama	dread	dream
harsh	haste	marsh	matter	metre
shade	shame	shard	share	smart
smear	stare	start	stash	steam
steer	tease	trade	trash	tread

6 Letters

arrest	dearth	hammer	hearse	master
seethe	stream	street	stress	trader

More

hamster   mattress   rehearse   stammer

All Letters: HEADMASTER

3 Letters

ear	eat	has	hat	rat	saw
sat	sea	see	set	she	sir
sit	tar	tea	the	wet	wit

4 Letters

ease	hair	hare	hart	hash	hate
hear	heat	hers	hiss	rash	rate
rest	sash	sear	seat	stew	stir
swat	tart	tear	teat	test	that
thaw	this	twit	wait	wart	wash
wear	west	what	whet	wish	with

5 Letters

haste	heart	heath	share	shear
sheet	shire	shirt	shrew	smash
stare	stash	steer	straw	swear
sweat	sweet	taste	tease	teeth
threw	trash	treat	twist	waist
waste	wheat	wrath	wrist	write

6 Letters and more

hearth	rather	sister	street	swathe
thirst	raisin	waiter	wither	weather
whether	sweater	heather	shatter	twitter

All Letters: SWEATSHIRT

OVER THE *M*OON   10

When you are over the moon, you are very pleased or happy about something.
If you have to pull your socks up, you have to become more efficient.
When you beat about the bush, you talk about something in an indirect way without coming to the point.
If you call it a day, you decide to bring something to an end or to stop.
When you jump a queue you move nearer to the front of a queue so that you reach the front before it is your turn.
Ray has tied himself in knots. – He is confused, anxious and nervous.
If you get something for a song, you get it cheaply.
The thief was caught red-handed. – He was caught while committing the crime.
If you drop a brick you say something tactless or inappropriate.
My wife has green fingers. – She is very good at gardening.
This man has been 'sent to Coventry'. – People refuse to speak to him.

TIME TO WRITE   11

1. I was **over the moon** when I passed . . .
2. Don't **beat about the bush**, tell me . . .
3. . . . you must really **pull your socks up** . . .
4. The burglar was **caught red-handed** . . .
5. I didn't realise . . . and so I **dropped a brick** . . .
6. . . . a field of weeds; Jim really has **green fingers**.
7. . . . my boyfriend and I decided to **call it a day** . .
8. Do you mind if I **jump the queue** . . .
9. I bought the plate **for a song** . . .
10. He was so nervous . . . and **tie himself in knots**.
11. . . . we decided to **send him to Coventry** . . .

*C*OOL *C*OLLOCATIONS   12

The **odd ones out** are:

1. an **answer**
2. an **idea**
3. **friends**
4. an **umbrella**
5. an **illusion**
6. a **promise**
7. your **homework**
8. a **computer**
9. **life**
10. a **party**
11. the **measles**
12. the **silence**
13. a **haircut**
14. a **question**
15. a **promise**
16. a **disappointment**

*E*URO-QUIZ   14

CITY	COUNTRY	LANGUAGE	ILLUSTRATIONS
1. Dublin	(Rep. of) Ireland	English / Irish Gaelic	1. England
2. Edinburgh	Scotland*	English / Scottish Gaelic	2. Spain
3. London	England*	English*	3. Italy
4. Amsterdam	Netherlands	Dutch	4. Switzerland
5. Copenhagen	Denmark	Danish	5. Germany
6. Gothenburg	Sweden	Swedish	6. France
7. Brussels	Belgium	Flemish / French	7. Scotland
8. Munich	Germany	German	
9. Vienna	Austria	German	
10. Berne	Switzerland	German / French / Italian / Rhaeto-Romanic	
11. Paris	France	French	
12. Lisbon	Portugal	Portuguese	
13. Madrid	Spain	Spanish	
14. Rome	Italy	Italian	

* While politically united as Great Britain within the UK, Scotland and England retain their status as different 'countries', as evidenced, e.g., on the occasion of football championships in which they take part with their own separate teams.
Member states of the European Union: Austria, Belgium, Britain, Denmark, Finland, France, Germany, Greece, Ireland, Italy, Luxembourg, Netherlands, Portugal, Spain, Sweden

Time for a Rhyme — 16

1. post – most
2. break – lake
3. week – speak
4. bread – red
5. heard – word
6. rose – chose
7. lose – choose
8. cow – plough
9. reign – stain
10. flood – mud
11. food – mood
12. done – won
13. foul – growl
14. lost – cost
15. pear – hare
16. hear – beer
17. five – alive
18. bowl – hole

Rhyme Groups — 17

break: ache, brake, shake, take
reign: gain, lane, rein, train
rose: flows, goes, toes

bowl: foal, goal, role, soul, toll
pear: flair, pair, share
lose: blues, brews, moose, shoes

heard: bird, herd, stirred
hear: dear, deer, peer, pier

Too Many Cooks / Proverbs — 18/19

1. Like father .... like son.
2. Love me .... love my dog.
3. Once bitten .... twice shy.
4. Strike .... while the iron is hot.
5. A creaking door .... hangs longest.
6. Still waters .... run deep.
7. Beauty .... is only skin deep.
8. Out of sight .... out of mind.
9. It takes all sorts .... to make a world.
10. An apple a day .... keeps the doctor away.
11. Speech is silver, ... silence is golden.
12. Half a loaf .... is better than none.
13. All's well that .... ends well.
14. Practice .... makes perfect.
15. Time and tide .... wait for no man.
16. Blood is .... thicker than water.

Relate the proverbs to the definitions

1. The proof of the pudding is in the eating.
2. As you make your bed, so you must lie in it.
3. Don't put all your eggs in one basket.
4. The grass is always greener on the other side . .
5. It's too late to shut the stable door after . . .
6. Don't cross a bridge until you come to it.
7. It's never too late to mend.
8. Absence makes the heart grow fonder.
9. Those (People) who live in glass houses . . .
10. Don't make a mountain out of a molehill.

Part and Parcel / Take Part in These Exercises — 20/21

1. A **thumb** is part of a hand.
2. A **branch** is part of a tree.
3. An **arm** is part of a body.
4. An **eye** is part of a face.
5. A **wing** is part of a bird.
6. An **elbow** is part of an arm.
7. An **aisle** is part of a church.
8. A **frame** is part of a picture.
9. A **toe** is part of a foot.
10. A **string** is part of a guitar.
11. A **button** is part of a shirt.
12. A **door** is part of a house.
13. A **chip** is part of a computer.
14. A **mattress** is part of a bed.
15. A **flowerbed** is part of a garden.
16. A **page** is part of a book.
17. A **sole** is part of a shoe.
18. A **knee** is part of a leg.
19. An **anchor** is part of a ship.
20. A **petal** is part of a flower.

1. The front **door** of the **house** . . .
2. The rear **garden** has a central **flowerbed** . . . an old apple **tree**. In the autumn the **branches** . . .
3. Your **hand** is the part of your **body**. . . end of your **arm** . . . a **thumb** . . . joined at the **elbow**.
4. There are five **toes** at the end of your **foot** . . . Your **knees** are halfway up your **legs** . . .
5. . . . Unfortunately the **soles** of his **shoes** . . . there were several **buttons** missing from his **shirt** . . .

How British Are You? — 23

1. Good morning, Claudia. Did you sleep well? .... Yes, thank you, very well. (8)
2. What would you like to drink? .... Tea, please. (7)
3. Could you pass the butter, please? .... Certainly, here you are. (9)
4. Would you like some more toast? .... No, thank you. I'm fine. (3)
5. I'm afraid I have broken a cup. I'm sorry. .... Oh, never mind about that, we'll replace it. (10)
6. May I have a front door key, please? .... Yes, of course, but don't lose it! (11)
7. Is it all right if I come home a bit later tonight? .... Yes, all right, but be home by 10 o'clock. (12)
8. May I borrow your dictionary? .... Yes, here you are. (2)
9. Do you mind if I watch television? .... No, not at all, go ahead. (6)
10. May I have something to drink, please? .... Yes, of course. Help yourself, there's plenty in the fridge. (5)
11. Have you got the time, please? .... I'm afraid I haven't. Sorry. (4)
12. I'm sorry I'm late. .... That's all right, but try to be punctual next time. (1)

Compose a Compound — 24

SOLID COMPOUNDS

skyscraper
blackbird
houseboat
grandfather
racehorse
watchdog
photocopy
motorway
handshake
streetlamp
newspaper
schoolboy
standpoint
snowflake
haircut
lipstick
earthquake

OPEN COMPOUNDS

parking ticket
car park
petrol station
pocket money
gold medal
status symbol
dance floor
ice cube
Prime Minister
tea break
junk food
CD player
youth club
table tennis
charter flight
registry office
phone call

Choose a Compound — 25

1. . . . **houseboat** to the sound of a **blackbird** . . .
2. The **schoolboy** did not enjoy having a **haircut**
3. . . . with a **handshake** and a **gold medal** . . .
4. . . . **youth club** . . . **table tennis** . . . **dance floor**
5. I need a **photocopy** . . . from the **registry office**
6. . . . **streetlamp** . . . **car park** . . . **parking ticket**
7. . . . **pocket money** my **grandfather** . . . **CD player**
8. . . .**standpoint** our government . . . the **earthquake**
9. . . .stopped at a **petrol station** . . . **motorway**
10. Our **watchdog** barked . . . steal our **racehorse**
11. **Snowflakes** began to settle . . . our **charter flight**
12. The **Prime Minister** received a **phone call** . . .

Synonyms — 26

brave – courageous
stubborn – obstinate
insane – mad
mean – stingy
giddy – dizzy
firm – solid
eager – keen
strong – powerful
fortunate – lucky
holy – sacred
relevant – pertinent
right – correct
huge – enormous
neat – tidy
careful – cautious

1. disappear – vanish
2. loathe – detest
3. alter – change
4. boast – brag
5. hide – conceal
6. help – assist
7. love – adore
8. answer – respond
9. admire – respect
10. beat – defeat
11. look – observe
12. hit – strike
13. swindle – deceive
14. build – construct
15. finish – cease

Synonym Quartets — 27

1. love, affection, fondness + **tenderness**
2. peace, agreement, unity + **harmony**
3. aid, help, protection + **support**
4. agreement, contract, deal + **arrangement**
5. danger, hazard, peril + **risk**
6. lie, falsehood, deception + **untruth**
7. consequence, effect, result + **outcome**
8. barrier, border, frontier + **boundary**
9. chat, conversation, conference + **talk**
10. contentment, bliss, pleasure + **happiness**
11. hatred, ill will, enmity + **dislike**
12. gift, grant, donation + **present**
13. fight, row, brawl + **quarrel**
14. bad luck, catastrophe, harm + **misfortune**
15. ache, distress, suffering + **pain**
16. vanity, pride, conceit + **arrogance**

Mixed Bag Quiz 28

A large store is divided into **departments.**

An American calls it a bill; in Britain it is a **banknote.**

When two colours go with each other, they **match.**

A person who is hopeful about . . . – **An optimist.**

The place where a river starts is its **source.**

The water in your mouth is called **saliva.**

Which word cannot describe an old person? – **Antique.**

Angry people sometimes **clench** their teeth.

When people meet again . . ., it's a **reunion.**

I hate doing my **homework** - especially maths.

The two holes in the nose are called **nostrils.**

If you hear of the late Mr May, you know he is **dead.**

Depth, height and width . . . **measurement.**

Tom drank too much . .. Now he has a **hangover.**

The time between night and day is called **dawn.**

Well-known in a negative way – **Notorious.**

. . . describe this facial expression? - A **grin.**

(a grin is a broad smile; also: to grin)

Link and Learn 29

H	E	Y	R	T
T	E	A	S	L
E	S	S	E	B
N	Y	R	I	K
O	M	G	C	S

B	I	R	A	T
L	O	T	H	N
A	N	R	D	E
D	T	Y	A	R
O	M	E	P	S

3 Letters

art, big, ear, cry, net, one
ray, rib, rig, say, sea, set
sir, tea, ten, try

4 Letters

bear, belt, best, crib, ease, easy
east, hear, kiss, less, nest, rear
rise, sick, tear, test, they, tray
year

5 Letters

beast, bless, easel, heart, lease, least
money, stray, tease, tense, these, treat
yeast, beast

6 Letters

bleary, crease, crisis, grease, hearse
lessen

More

hearsay, heartless, heartlessness

3 Letters

and, ant, bit, day, den, dot
dry, ear, far, had, hat, hen
lot, not, pay, pea, pet, rap
rat, ray, red, rob, rot, sap
say, spy, tan, ton, try, yap

4 Letters

blot, born, dare, darn, dent, dome
hand, head, heap, land, load, loan
lord, near, part, pear, pray, rare
rasp, rear, rent, riot, road, rota
that, toad, tome, trap, type, year

5 Letters

birth, bland, blond, drape, dread, modal
north, spade, spare, spear, spray, trade

6 Letters

blithe, border, endear, parade, rather

More birthday, spartan

Sort out the Sport — 30

1. baseball
2. ice-skating
3. hurdle race, hurdles
4. jogging / running
5. martial arts / karate
6. badminton
7. ski jumping
8. football
9. ice-hockey
10. parachuting
11. horse riding
12. windsurfing
13. scuba diving
14. basketball

Sort out the Sport — 31

team: football, basketball, ice-hockey, baseball
water sports: scuba diving, windsurfing
aerial sports: parachuting
winter sports: ski jumping, ice-skating, ice-hockey
equestrian sports: horse riding
athletics: hurdle race, hurdles, jogging / running
combat sports: karate

RELATE THE WORDS . . .

Riding: boots, hat/helmet, reins, saddle, stirrup
Athletics: bar, lane, ring, track
tennis: ballboy, net, racquet, serve
Skiing: boots, helmet, pole, ski, skiing goggles
Scuba Diving: air tank, flipper, mask, wet suit
Baseball: bat, glove, helmet, (face) mask, shin guard

Ups and Downs — 32

1. The Mays … are **selling up** their shop.
2. You can't just **let** me **down** now.
3. **Eat up** your dinner first, …
4. You must **cut down** on alcohol and fat, …
5. The police managed to **track down** the prisoner.
6. I just have to **do up** my shoe laces.
7. Don't **give up**. There is still hope …
8. **Slow down!** You're driving much too fast.
9. They tried to **hush up** the scandal, …
10. Don't **talk down** to me as if I was a child.
11. If this rainy weather **keeps up**, …
12. It's a pity that they had to **chop down** that tree.

Pair them Up — 33

explode – **blow up**
wear smarter clothes than usual – **dress up**
get out of bed – **get up**
clean the dishes – **wash up**
become adult – **grow up**
make a mistake – **slip up**
describe as less important – **play down**
put it into written form – **write down**
relax – **wind down**
stop functioning – **break down**
refuse – **turn down**
make oneself comfortable – **settle down**

Homophones — 34

ate – **eight**
bear – **bare**
blew – **blue**
break – **brake**
buy – **by**

flower – **flour**
hare – **hair**
herd – **heard**
here – **hear**
knew – **new**

knows – **nose**
male – **mail**
not – **knot**
one – **won**
plane – **plain**

right – **write**
seen – **scene**
sun – **son**
too – **two**
week – **weak**

1. I can't **bear** my husband walking in his **bare** feet indoors.
2. Luckily the garage fixed the faulty **brake** during my lunch **break**.
3. Everybody **knows** that Jim has always got his **nose** in a book.
4. He **knew** that my dress was **new** but he didn't say anything.
5. Liverpool **won** the match by **one** to nil.
6. I kept telling my teenage **son** to stay out of the **sun** but he wouldn't listen. **By** tomorrow morning he will have to **buy** some nice, soothing lotion!

Odd One Out   35

○ bow	○ bread	○ done	○ made
✗ cow	○ shed	○ one	○ shade
○ sew	○ led	○ won	✗ said
○ blow	✗ greed	✗ bone	○ maid

○ food	○ no	○ goes	○ load
✗ hood	○ so	✗ does	✗ broad
○ sued	✗ to	○ mows	○ mowed
○ rude	○ know	○ close	○ rode

○ coal	○ bird	○ bed	○ pair
✗ foul	○ heard	✗ bead	○ pear
○ soul	✗ ford	○ dead	✗ peer
○ roll	○ word	○ bread	○ dare

○ bake	○ crown	○ great	○ meat
○ brake	✗ flown	○ late	○ heat
✗ beak	○ noun	✗ greet	✗ threat
○ break	○ clown	○ grate	○ sweet

○ know	○ bun	○ tough	○ flower
✗ now	○ son	✗ though	○ flour
○ toe	✗ gone	○ enough	○ power
○ low	○ done	○ rough	✗ lower

○ heart	○ through	○ rose	○ foul
✗ heard	✗ cough	○ chose	✗ bowl
○ hart	○ shoe	✗ choose	○ owl
○ cart	○ flew	○ goes	○ growl

Super Similes   36

1. As free as **a bird**
2. As pretty as **a picture**
3. As good as **gold**
4. As quick as **lightning**
5. As sober as **a judge**
6. As strong as **a horse**
7. As thin as **a rake**
8. As poor as **a church mouse**
9. As light as **a feather**
10. As clear as **a bell**

More Similes   37

1. ... Now my tyre is as **flat as a pancake**.
2. ... you'll have to shout! She's as **deaf as a post**.
3. They're **as different as chalk and cheese**. ..., however, are **as like as two peas in a pod**.
4. ... that joke is **as old as the hills**.
5. ... It's **as silent as the grave** in here.
6. ... You've been as **miserable as sin** ...
7. ... but his hand was **as steady as a rock**.
8. ... Diann, who was **as fresh as a daisy**.
9. ... my father – he's as **hard as nails**.
10. ... years to come. He's **as tough as old boots**.
11. ... My new coat keeps me **as warm as toast**.

Antonyms   38

1. The **rich** countries should help the **poor** ones.
2. Don't stay up too **late** in the evening, if you have to get up **early** in the morning.
3. I told him I could only afford a **cheap** car, but he tried to sell me an **expensive** one.
4. I don't like **noisy** neighbours because I am a **quiet** person myself.
5. I got so **wet** in the rain that it took an hour to get **dry** again.
6. The water is quite **shallow** near the beach, but it gets **deep** very quickly.
7. I said I wanted a **hard**-boiled egg, but they gave me one that was **soft**-boiled.
8. Basketball players are usually very **tall**, you never see a **short** player.
9. Everybody had got up and was wide **awake**, only Harold was still fast **asleep**.
10. I can't believe that Sue is **ill**; she was perfectly **fine / healthy** when I last saw her.
11. A cobra can be **dangerous**, but most snakes are quite **harmless**.
12. Eagles have become **rare** in Europe, but blackbirds are quite **common**.
13. The train was rather **full** when we left, but after a couple of stops it got quite **empty**.
14. I'm used to our old **slow** car, John's Jaguar is much too **fast** for me.
15. They say that a clown's **happy** face quite often hides a **sad** person.
16. Tom is used to **weak** coffee, so Pam's espresso was much too **strong** for him.

OPPOSITES

answer – **question**	end – **beginning**	giant – **dwarf**	past – **future**
day – **night**	enemy – **friend**	hate – **love**	solution – **problem**
defeat – **victory**	evening – **morning**	hell – **heaven**	top – **bottom**
despair – **hope**	exit – **entrance**	loss – **profit**	war – **peace**

1. . . . from a state of **loss** into one of **profit**.
2. . . . almost certain **defeat** into a great **victory**.
3. . . . forget about the **past** and look to the **future**.
4. . . . through the **entrance** . . . leave by the **exit**.
5. . . . a **dwarf** standing beside Tom, a **giant** of . .
6. . . . end of the **war** in order to ensure **peace**.
7. . . . from the **beginning** . . . you reach the **end**.
8. Their **hope** of happiness turned into **despair** . .
9. . . . is their idea of **hell** but for me it's **heaven**.

WHAT'S UP?

1. . . . people always **mix** them **up**.
2. We . . . can easily **put** you **up**.
3. The inmates . . . are all **locked up** for the night.
4. . . . but we soon **caught up** with him.
5. . . . I will **pick** you **up** in my car.
6. Before a race an athlete needs to **warm up**.
7. . . . You are not allowed to **light up** here.
8. . . . is so late. It always **messes up** our plans.
9. Tim would have **cracked up** under the strain. . .
10. Please **speak up**. I can't understand you.
11. . . . sports instructor. He will **fix** you **up** . . .
12. . . . difficult words! I'll have to **look** them **up** . . .
13. . . . I think he has just **made up** everything.
14. I have finally managed to **give up** smoking.
15. . . . you never have to **wind** them **up**.
16. The government have **set up** a committee . . .

IN A CLASS OF ITS OWN!

Rose, tulip . . .	=	FLO **W** ER
Uncle, cousin . . .	=	REL **A** TIVES
Bee, ant . . .	=	IN **S** ECTS
Shirt, jeans . . .	=	CLOT **H** ES
Europe, Asia . .	=	CONT **I** NENTS
Chair, table . . .	=	FUR **N** ITURE
Carrot, celery . .	=	VE **G** ETABLES
Oak, fir . . .	=	**T** REES
GB, Italy . . .	=	C **O** UNTRIES
Earth . . .	=	PLA **N** ETS

Church . . .	=	BUI **L** DINGS
Lion, pig . . .	=	ANIM **A** LS
Everest, Etna . . .	=	MOU **N** TAINS
Suitcase, bag . . .	=	LU **G** GAGE
Orange, pear . . .	=	FR **U** IT
Atlantic . . .	=	OCE **A** NS
English . . .	=	LAN **G** UAGES
Polo, chess . . .	=	GAM **E** S
London . . .	=	**C** ITIES
Football . . .	=	SP **O** RTS
Red, mauve . . .	=	COLO **U** RS
Rhine . . .	=	**R** IVERS
To call . . .	=	VERB **S**
Theft, murder . . .	=	CRIM **E** S

SHARED BEGINNINGS

light	– bulb	– house	– switch
hand	– bag	– shake	– book
land	– mark	– scape	– slide
door	– bell	– mat	– step
water	– colour	– fall	– front

fire	– place	– man	– arm
sun	– bed	– light	– beam
night	– club	– dress	– mare
book	– shelf	– worm	– mark
head	– master	– phones	– line

life	– boat	– belt	– style
bread	– crumb	– winner	– bin
road	– block	– side	– works
milk	– man	– shake	– tooth
house	– hold	– maid	– boat

1. . . . new **lighthouse** . . an interesting **landmark**
2. . . . newspaper **headline** . . in a local **nightclub**.
3. The **fireman/headmaster** . . . an extravagant **lifestyle** . . . as he was the only **breadwinner**.
4. The **milkman** . . . the milk on the **doorstep** . . .
5. . . . bright **sunlight** . . . dust on the **bookshelf** . .
6. . . . the **doorbell** . . . visitor with a **handshake**.
7. . . . have a **housemaid** to answer the **doorbell**.
8. The **lifeboat** crew threw a **lifebelt** to the . . .
9. . . . **roadworks** are proving to be a **nightmare** . .

LAND MARKS 44

Loch Ness
Mount Everest
Niagara Falls
Piccadilly Circus
The River Rhine
The Tower of London
The Swiss Alps

The Atlantic Ocean
The British Isles
The Cape of Good Hope
The Isle of Wight
The Mississippi Delta
The North Pole
The Panama Canal

The Arctic Circle
The Rocky Mountains
The Scottish Highlands
The Statue of Liberty
The Strait of Gibraltar
South Africa

ANIMAL IDIOMS 46

If you hear something **straight from the horse's mouth**, you hear it from someone in a position to know it is true.
Greg has **gone to the dogs**. – Greg has let himself go morally or physically.
If something is **dead as a dodo**, it is no longer in fashion or no longer exists.
If you've had **a whale of a time**, you have enjoyed yourself very much.
A **wolf in sheep's clothing** is a person who acts like a friend, but is hiding his unfriendly intentions.
When you **smell a rat**, you suspect something is wrong
Sam had to do all the **donkey work** at his office. – Sam had to do the least important and most unpleasant tasks.
Alf had **other fish to fry**. – Alf had other, more important things to do.
If you buy **a pig in a poke**, you buy something without seeing it or without knowing its value.
If somebody **makes a pig of himself**, he eats far too much and greedily.
Renovating this house would be a **mammoth task**. – It is a very large job needing a lot of effort.
If you **let the cat out of the bag**, you give away a secret.
Grandfather grinned like a **Cheshire cat**. – He had a wide smile all over his face.
Sheila had **butterflies in her stomach**. – She felt nervous.
Look what the cat's brought in! – You are surprised and pleased to see someone!
If you say that someone or something is a **sitting duck**, you mean that they are easy to attack or harm.
Making a **beeline** for something means to go quickly or by the shortest way towards something.

LOOK IN THE RIGHT PLACE 48

1. article – **newspaper**
2. teacher – **school**
3. waiter – **restaurant**
4. seat belt – **car**
5. violinist – **orchestra**
6. shower – **bathroom**
7. clown – **circus**
8. page – **book**
9. altar – **church**
10. cook – **kitchen**
11. transit lounge – **airport**
12. secretary – **office**
13. cell – **prison**
14. actor – **theatre**
15. king – **palace**
16. pilot – **aeroplane**

FALLING INTO PLACE 49

AEROPLANE – cockpit, flight attendant
AIRPORT – check-in counter, departure gate
BATHROOM – towel rail, washbasin
BOOK – illustration, index
CAR – dashboard, speedometer, steering wheel
CHURCH – congregation, vicar, pulpit
CIRCUS – acrobat, lion-tamer, ringmaster
KITCHEN – cooker, saucepan
PRISON – inmate, warden
NEWSPAPER – editorial, headline
OFFICE – filing cabinet, photocopier
ORCHESTRA – conductor, musician
PALACE – servants, throne
RESTAURANT – dessert trolley, menu
SCHOOL – blackboard, headmaster
THEATRE – box office, stage

Don't Count Your Chickens... 50

If you put the cart before the horse, you deal with things in the wrong order.
You can't teach an old dog new tricks! – Some people, especially old people, don't like to try new ways of doing things.
Don't count your chickens before they're hatched! – Don't be over-optimistic or over-confident of success!
A leopard never changes its spots, means that somebody's basic nature never changes.
If you have too many irons in the fire, you are involved in too many different activities at the same time.
You can take a horse to water, but you cannot make him drink. – You can try to convince or persuade people, but you cannot force them to do something they don't want to do.

1. **Learn to walk before you run.** – You cannot be perfect at once, but must learn things gradually.
2. **It never rains but it pours.** – Misfortunes often come together.
3. **You can't have your cake and eat it.** – You have to choose between two alternatives and cannot pick what suits you from each.
4. **Many hands make light work.** – If many people work together and complement each other, the task will be completed more quickly and more easily.

1. **Look before you leap.** – Think ahead and consider the consequences of what you are about to do.
2. **All that glitters is not gold.** – A pleasing outward appearance does not mean that the thing or person has real value.
3. **A burnt child dreads the fire.** – A negative experience makes you more careful the next time you are in a similar situation.
4. **Better be safe than sorry.** – Rather than do something you may regret, it is better to take every possible precaution, even if it seems unnecessary.

Look for Links 52

1. Hunger is to eat as thirst is to . . . **drink**.
2. Leather is to shoe as wool is to . . . **jumper**.
3. Sight is to eyes as smell is to . . . **nose**.
4. Leg is to knee as arm is to . . . **elbow**.
5. Aunt is to niece as uncle is to . . . **nephew**.
6. Roof is to house as ceiling is to . . . **room**.
7. Cat is to animal as fly is to . . . **insect**.
8. Ear is to hear as eye is to . . . **see**.
9. Man is to foot as cat is to . . . **paw**.
10. Opera is to sing as theatre is to . . . **act**.
11. Woman is to wife as man is to . . . **husband**.
12. Light is to dark as happy is to . . . **sad**.
13. Cat is to kitten as horse is to . . . **foal**.
14. Wood is to tree as wool is to . . . **sheep**.
15. Bread is to baker as clothes are to . . . **tailor**.
16. Pig is to grunt as cow is to . . . **moo**.

Fill That Gap 53

Here are some examples of possible words:

— et	bet	get	jet	let	met	net	pet	set	vet	wet	yet
diet	feet	fret	meet	fleet	greet	sleet	sweet	valet	mallet	ballet	
claret	pocket	packet	socket	street	discreet						

— at	bat	cat	eat	fat	hat	mat	pat	rat	sat	tat	vat
beat	boat	feat	heat	meat	neat	peat	pleat	prat	seat	that	
bleat	carat	cheat	treat	wheat	combat	cravat	repeat	mistreat			

— ill	bill	dill	fill	gill	hill	kill	mill	pill	sill	till
will	quill	refill	uphill	downhill						

Vexing Vowels 55

beat / iː /	hear / ɪə /	head / ɛ /	learn / ɜː /
appeal	beard	bread	early
cheat	clear	breakfast	earn
east	ear	breath	earth
peace	fear	feather	heard
sea	real	health	pearl

Same sound – spelled differently

beat / iː /	hear / ɪə /	head / ɛ /	learn / ɜː /
feet	beer	bell	bird
flea	dear	dead	burn
heap	deer	red	herd
niece	here	said	hurt
piece	pier	tread	word

It's How You Say It! 56

1. 'Oh, I'm very sorry,' Tom **apologised**.
2. 'Where did you buy that car?' my friend **asked**.
3. '. . . better than M. Jackson,' Clum C. **boasted**.
4. 'Get out of my garden,' the man **shouted**.
5. 'I will always love you,' the husband **vowed**.
6. 'This music is much too loud,' they **complained**.
7. 'This man was poisoned,' Holmes **concluded**.
8. 'It was me who broke that cup,' S. **admitted**.
9. 'Pssst! Don't wake up the baby,' she **whispered**.
10. 'Don't touch that cat . . .,' Melissa **warned**.
11. 'Right then, I will take the green sofa,' he **decided**.
12. '. . . a Rubens painting,' the collector **exclaimed**.
13. '. . . till six o'clock,' the officer **commanded**.
14. '. . . the test on Tuesday,' the teacher **announced**.
15. 'I will wash the car for you,' A. **volunteered**.

Supply sentences that go with the reporting verbs 57

Here are some suggestions

1. **'Please, can we go to the zoo?'** the child begged.
2. **'If you wash the car, you can have it on Sunday,'** Dad promised.
3. **'Has the government decided on a new strategy?'** the reporter wanted to know.
4. **'Thanks for the invitation, I'll definitely be there,'** he accepted.
5. **'Investment in computer technology will continue to grow,'** the expert predicted.
6. **'Let's go to the cinema tonight,'** Ryan suggested.
7. **'If you don't get your act together, you'll be in trouble,'** the teacher warned Keith.
8. **'Oh, no. Not another one of those stupid chat shows on TV,'** my father groaned.
9. **'Take one of these pills every morning and the pain will go away,'** the doctor explained.
10. **'I can give you a lift in my car,'** Tony offered.
11. **'Please forgive me, . . . I didn't mean to . . . , I'm sorry,'** he gulped.
12. **'Don't forget your packed lunches,'** mother reminded us.
13. **'We apprehended these two car thieves in the car park,'** the policeman reported.
14. **'Don't worry, I am a policeman,'** the detective assured the old lady.
15. **'We will be landing shortly,'** the pilot informed the passengers.

Scrabble 58

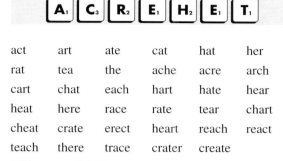

act	art	ate	cat	hat	her
rat	tea	the	ache	acre	arch
cart	chat	each	hart	hate	hear
heat	here	race	rate	tear	chart
cheat	crate	erect	heart	reach	react
teach	there	trace	crater	create	

All Letters: TEACHER

eat	fit	lea	lit	sit	tea
vat	ease	fail	file	fist	five
flea	life	lift	list	live	safe
save	tail	vase	vast	veal	veil
vial	seal	salt	silt	alive	false
feast	least	slave	stale	valet	slate

All Letters: FESTIVAL

ace	act	ant	can	cat	net
ran	rat	tan	tar	ten	tin
acne	acre	cart	neat	nice	race
rain	rate	rent	rice	tear	react
create	trace	train	inert	crane	trance
nectar					

All Letters: CERTAIN

aim	arm	can	car	man	ram
ran	rim	clam	cram	mail	main
nail	rail	rain	claim		

All Letters: CRIMINAL

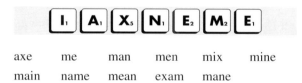

axe	me	man	men	mix	mine
main	name	mean	exam	mane	

All Letters: EXAMINE

age	bag	bat	bee	eat	eel
eve	get	lee	leg	let	tab
tag	tea	vat	able	bale	beat
gale	gave	glee	late	tale	vale
veal	table	gable	bleat	leave	valet

All Letters: VEGETABLE

Be as good as your Word / Even better ... 60/61

1. Ray has no money. He is **broke**.
2. Let me **carry** your bag for you.
3. London has about 7 million **inhabitants**.
4. She is going to **make** coffee for all of us.
5. When you buy something you often get a **receipt**.
6. Vegetarians don't eat **meat**.
7. Nobody is perfect. We all make **mistakes**.
8. Dad is always on time. He's so **punctual**.
9. We went to see a football **match** yesterday.
10. Dad has no hair on his head. He is **bald**.
11. The Rhine is Germany's longest **river**.
12. Anne can't hear. She is **deaf**.
13. She wears a gold **watch** on her wrist.
14. Can you **teach** me to play the piano?
15. Could you **lend** me a pound, please?
16. Let's have a **break** for lunch!

1. Her face went **blank**.
2. I really love to **wear** pure woollen jumpers.
3. The pillar has to be strong enough to **bear** ...
4. When the water starts to **boil** you can add ...
5. She paid a **deposit** towards the cost ...
6. ... it was only a **flesh** wound ...
7. A power **failure** caused the town ...
8. ... bill, Jane decided to make a **timely** exit.
9. ... stayed indoors and played a **game** of cards.
10. The **bold** soldier went into battle ...
11. When the river began to **flood** ...
12. She was struck **dumb** with fright ...
13. ... a large gold **clock** on the mantelpiece.
14. It's not easy to **learn** a new language.
15. May I **borrow** £5 if I promise to repay ...
16. ... without taking a **pause** for breath.
17. During the **interval** we went for a drink ...

Dial a Word 62

Here are some examples of possible words:

3 Letters

bar	bat	cab	car	cat	ear
eat	let	rat	tab	tar	tea

4 Letters

able	acre	bale	bare	bear	beer
beat	brat	care	cart	crab	lace
late	race	rate	real	reel	tact
tale	tear				

5 and more Letters

cable	cater	clear	crate	elect	label
react	table	treat	trace	brace	ballet
berate	career	cereal	claret	crater	create
rebate	relate	tablet	treacle	bracelet	
lacerate					

All Letters: CELEBRATE

3 Letters

den	die	eel	hen	led	lee
sea	see	she			

4 Letters

Dane	dead	deal	dean	deed	dine
ease	head	heal	heed	held	heel
hell	hide	idle	lane	lead	lean
lend	lens	line	need	sale	sane
seal	seed	sell	send	side	shed

5 and more Letters

dense	ladle	lease	leash
lense	linen	shade	shale
sheen	shine	slide	handle
hassle	lessen	needle	senile
saddle	sailed	slash	nailed

All Letters: HEADLINES

Famous last Words 63

—— oo ——

4 Letters

book	boom	boon	boot	cook	cool
coot	doom	door	food	fool	foot
good	hood	hoof	hook	hoot	look
loom	loot	mood	moon	moor	nook
noon	pool	poor	roof	rook	room
root	soot	took	toot		

5 Letters

aloof	blood	boost	booth	booty	booze
brood	broom	flood	floor	gloom	goose
groom	loose	moose	noose	proof	roost
shoot	spool	swoon	tooth		

6 and more Letters

baboon	choose	doodle	groove
hoover	noodle	poodle	racoon
school	balloon	pontoon	rooster
scooter	hooligan	bamboozle	boomerang

—— ee ——

4 Letters

beep	beer	beet	deed	deep	deer
feed	feet	flee	free	heed	heel
leek	meet	need	peel	peep	peer
reel	seed	seem	seep	seer	weep

5 Letters

agree	bleep	breed	fleet	greed	seedy
sheep	sheer	sheet	sleep	steep	steer
teeth					

6 and more Letters

beetle	breeze	career	feeble
fleece	freeze	needle	seethe
sleeve	street	freedom	feeling
greeting	meeting	agreement	

—— ie ——

4 Letters
diet   pier   tier

5 Letters
cried   field   fiend   fiery   niece   piece
piety   siege   sieve   spied   tried

6 Letters
belief   fierce   fiesta   friend   grieve   pierce
relief

More   ancient   believe   cashier   glacier
piebald   relieve   science   retrieve   efficient
chandelier   hierarchy
hieroglyph   lieutenant

—— ay ——

3 Letters
bay   day   fay   gay   hay   jay
lay   may   pay   ray   say   way

4 Letters
bray   clay   dray   flay   fray   fray
play   pray   stay   tray

5 Letters
array   foray   relay   stray   spray

More   betray   hooray   defray   dismay
outlay   waylay   hooray   display   hearsay
disarray

—— ate ——

4 Letters
bate   date   fate   gate   hate   late
mate   rate   sate

5 Letters
abate   crate   grate   plate   slate   spate
state

6 Letters
create   donate   rebate   relate

More   operate   mediate   deflate
dominate   inflate   considerate   moderate
degenerate   domesticate   exaggerate   confederate
generate   illiterate   corroborate   navigate
recuperate   magistrate

—— eat ——

beat   feat   heat   meat   neat
peat   seat   bleat   cheat   great
pleat   treat   wheat   defeat   repeat
threat   retreat   entreat   mistreat

INCREASE YOUR WORDPOWER • KEY

INCREASE YOUR WORDPOWER 2 • Key

How Do you Do?	23
When the Cat's away	23
Confusable Verbs	23
Keep your Fingers Crossed	24
Body Language	25
Wordpower Rockets	25
In a Class of its Own	26
Time for a Rhyme / Odd One Out	26
Super-duper razzmatazz	26
Star Characters	27
Compose a Compound	27
Word Pyramids	27
Synonyms	27
Synonym Quartets	28
Hair-raising Synonyms	28
Of Compounds	28
Looking Good	29
Homographs	29
Homophones	30
For better for worse / Antonyms	30
Double Antonyms	30
Making Headlines	31
Confusable Adjectives	31
Made in America	32
What's Cooking?	32
Now you're Talking	33
Mixed Bag Quiz	34
Look for Links	35
Look in the right Place	35
Landmarks	35
Know the Ins and Outs	35
Get your Teeth into Colloquial English	36
Just like a Bull in a China Shop / Idioms of Comparison	36
Fixed Phrases	37
Up or Down?	38
All's Well that Ends Well	38
Ladies & Gentlemen	38
Add your Ad	39
Who is Who?	39
Gerund Compounds	40
American & British English	40
Confusable Nouns	40
Be as good as your Word	42
The Golden Middle	42
Professional Compounds	42
When all is said and done	43
Quantities	43
Scrabble	44
Fixed Phrases	44
Dial A word	46

How do you do? 5

1. Thank you for all your help. – **Not at all.**
2. I won £ 800 in the National Lottery last Saturday. – **Congratulations.**
3. I can't stand greasy food. – **Neither can I.**
4. Do you think this rain will stop soon? – **I certainly hope so.**
5. I'm sorry about having lost your pen. – **Oh, never mind.**
6. Have a nice weekend. – **Thanks. The same to you.**
7. Hello, how are you? – **I'm fine, thanks, and you?**
8. I'm sitting my final exam tomorrow. – **Good luck!**
9. Excuse me, but you are standing on my foot. – **Oh, I'm sorry.**
10. Can I help you with this suitcase? – **That's very kind of you, thank you.**
11. Have you met my old friend Mark? – **Pleased to meet you. I'm John.**
12. Would you like a cup of tea? – **Yes, please. / No, thank you.**

When the Cat's Away 6

1. As you sow .... so you reap.
2. A stitch in time .... saves nine.
3. You win some .... you lose some.
4. He who laughs last ...... laughs longest.
5. One good turn .... deserves another.
6. Live .... and let live.
7. Great minds .... think alike.
8. A new broom .... sweeps clean.
9. Beggars .... can't be choosers.
10. Pigs .... might fly!
11. It's no use .... crying over spilt milk.
12. Nothing ventured .... nothing gained.
13. Actions .... speak louder than words.
14. A fool and his money . are soon parted.

... and Pigs Might Fly! 7

1. . . . you never know, **pigs might fly.**
2. . . . besides, **beggars can't be choosers.**
3. . . . after all, **every dog has its day.**
4. . . . you were young once; so **live and let live.**
5. . . . say, **never judge a book by its cover.**
6. . . . my advice is **look before you leap.**
7. . . . what they say: **it never rains but it pours.**
8. . . . However, **it's no use crying over spilt milk.**
9. . . . **where there's a will, there's a way.**
10. . . . **When the cat's away, the mice will play.**

Confusable Verbs 8

1. What did your wife **say** when you **told** her . . .?
2. Could you **make** a birthday cake for Christine?
3. I will **lend** you two pounds, if you give me . . .
4. Tom **took** Janet to the cinema last night.
5. Don't **lie** in bed all morning. Get up!
6. I wouldn't **say** no to a glass of beer or two.
7. I told her four times, but she wasn't **listening**!
8. I'll **make** you a nice cup of tea.
9. The neighbour's cat has been **watching** . . .
10. We can **go up** in the elevator . . .
11. May I **borrow** your English dictionary, please?
12. When you come here, please **bring** your books.
13. He **listened**, but couldn't **hear** everything.
14. He **laid** his coat . . . paper which was **lying** there.
15. I usually **get up** at 8.30 in the morning.
16. She **told** us she would go home.
17. He **did** his best, but he still **made** . . . mistakes.
18. Please **take** this letter . . . and **bring** me . . .
19. I have never **seen** a bird like that before!
20. How many eggs does this hen **lay** each week?
21. I didn't have time to **make** the beds.
22. . . . **watching** the crowd, when he **saw** his wife .

Confusable Verbs

Choose the correct word, then write a sentence containing the alternative word . . . / Suggestions and definitions

1. I'm late, I shall have to **go** by taxi. / Can I **drive** you to the station?
   To go: general expression, sometimes with an additional 'by train, by bus, by car etc.' • **To drive**: to act as a driver

2. At what age do babies learn to **walk**? / Let's **go** to the disco tonight!
   To go: to move or be in motion, travel • **To walk**: to move along on foot

3. He has managed to **save** enough . . . / Please **spare** me your explanations!
   To save: to keep something for the future so that it will be available when you need it
   To spare: to refrain from inflicting something unpleasant on someone

4. Who **invented** the telephone? / Columbus **discovered** America in 1492.
   To invent: to be the first person to think of something, to create something
   To discover: to be the first person to find a place, substance or fact which nobody knew about before

5. Mr Briton **carries** an umbrella... / I can't **bear** my brother-in-law! / This document **bears** your signature.
   To carry: to take from one place to another; to have with one • **To bear**: to put up with or endure, to have or show

6. Would you **draw** the curtains, please? / This naughty boy keeps **pulling** my hair!
   To draw: to pull along, across, forward or towards you • **To pull**: stronger than draw, often implies force and effort

7. I think I **left** my handbag **behind** at the theatre last night. / Don't **forget** to take your raincoat.
   To leave behind: to forget to take it with you when you go away from a place
   To forget: to not remember to take something with you when you go somewhere

8. Could you **remind** me to phone ..? / Do you **remember** where I put the key?
   To remind: to cause somebody to remember to do something • **To remember**: to keep in mind or bring back to mind

9. I shall have to have it **altered**. . . / I took the black dress back to the shop and **changed** it for a white one.
   To change: to replace it or to get something of a similar kind • **To alter**: to change partially in form, character or position

10. I like you in that colour, it really **suits** you . . . / I like you in that jumper, does it **fit** properly?
    To suit: if something suits you it makes you look good and attractive • **To fit**: if something fits it's the right size

11. We saw Karajan **conducting** . . . / I asked Kenneth Branagh to **direct** Hamlet at the National Theatre.
    To conduct: a conductor stands in front of an orchestra and conducts its members
    To direct: the director of a film or a play is in charge of it and organises the way it is made and performed

12. Didn't you **notice** what she was wearing? / 'You look really well,' he **remarked**.
    To notice: to become aware of something • **To remark**: to say what you think about something or noticed about someone

13. Are you going to **spend** a long time in the States? / I brought a book along to **pass** the time.
    To spend time: you spend time in a place if you're there from the beginning to the end of that period of time
    To pass the time: to have something to occupy yourself with while waiting for something

14. Who **taught** you to play the piano so well? / I **learnt** how to write when I was four years old.
    To teach: to explain a subject to a pupil as a teacher or show someone how to do a particular task
    To learn: to get knowledge of something or skill in doing it by your own efforts or hard work

Keep Your Fingers Crossed

We'll keep our fingers crossed for you. – We'll hope for a good result and good luck.

John didn't have a leg to stand on. – John had no excuse for his actions or views.

The thief took to his heels when he saw the policeman. – The thief ran away when he saw the policeman coming.

George waited on his wife hand and foot. – He did everything his wife wanted.

If you poke your nose into something, you – interfere with something even though it doesn't concern you.

My ears are burning! – Someone must be talking about me.

Mark and Tom are always at loggerheads with each other. – They always disagree very strongly with each other.

Russell has a sweet tooth. – He likes to eat sweet things.

Melanie is the apple of her mother's eye. – Mum is very fond of Melanie.

BODY LANGUAGE 11

1. Peter . . . **was ill in bed** for several weeks.
2. I **feel sure** that Anne is the right girl for me.
3. I'll **look after** the baby while you're out . . .
4. . . . **you said exactly what I was about to say.**
5. James . . . **likes to meet and talk to** rich people.
6. **likes to be involved in everything that happens.**
7. . . . it was difficult for us **to remain serious**.
8. We shall **be very busy** when our visitors arrive . .
9. . . . You look **unhappy and miserable** today.
10. . . . is **very kind and considerate to other people**.
11. I was **trying very hard to think of** something . .
12. . . . **would be willing to do almost anything** . .

WORDPOWER ROCKETS 12

Here are some examples of possible words:

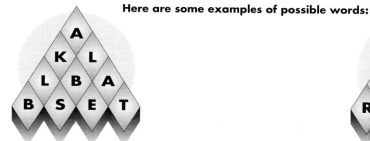

3 Letters

all	ask	bat	bee	bet	eat
eel	lee	let	sat	sea	see
set	tab	tea	tee		

4 Letters

able	bake	ball	base	bask	beak
beat	bell	belt	best	lake	late
leak	leek	sake	seat	seek	sell
take	talk	tall	task	teak	tell

5 Letters

beast	blast	bleak	bleat	label	least
skate	slake	sleek	stake	stale	stalk
stall	state	steak	steal	steel	table
taste	tease				

6 Letters and more

| babble | ballet | basket | battle | latest |
| stable | tablet | ballast | baseball | |

All Letters: BASKETBALL

3 Letters

ace	ant	cad	cat	cod	con
cot	din	don	dot	eat	ice
ire	net	nod	nor	not	ran
rat	rot	tan	tar	tea	tee
ten	tin	ton	tor		

4 Letters

card	care	cart	coat	code	coin
cord	core	dare	date	dead	dear
deed	deer	dent	dice	dine	door
iron	neat	nice	race	raid	rain
rant	rare	rate	read	rein	rend
rent	rice	ride	riot	road	roar
tear	tend	tent	toad		

5 Letters

adore	carat	crate	dance	decor	drain
dread	drone	enact	inter	react	rotor
trace	tract	trade	train	tread	trend

6 Letters and more

accent	accord	anoint	attend	career
carrot	carton	cordon	crater	create
credit	decant	direct	endear	nation
notion	ornate	ration	recant	recede
record	render	rotate	tender	tinder
carrion	cartoon	oration	tractor	treacle
decorate	donation	nicotine	reindeer	

All Letters: DECORATION

IN A CLASS OF ITS OWN!   13

Breakfast . . .	=	MEAL **S**		General . . .	=	OFFI **C** ERS
Eel, shark . . .	=	FIS **H** ES		Love, hate . . .	=	FE **E** LINGS
Wheat, barley . . .	=	CERE **A** LS		Ring . . .	=	JEWE **L** LERY
Tea, whiskey . . .	=	DRIN **K** S		Cholera . . .	=	DIS **E** ASES
Knives, forks . . .	=	CUTL **E** RY		One, eight . . .	=	NUM **B** ERS
Bible, guide . . .	=	BOOK **S**		Kitchen . . .	=	**R** OOMS
Rome . . .	=	CA **P** ITALS		British . . .	=	NATION **A** LITIES
Dollar, yen . . .	=	CURR **E** NCIES		Asia . . .	=	CON **T** INENTS
Iron, copper . . .	=	MET **A** LS		Christianity, . . .	=	REL **I** GIONS
Truly, sadly . . .	=	ADVE **R** BS		Basketball, . . .	=	SP **O** RTS
Susan . . .	=	NAM **E** S		Tango . . .	=	DA **N** CES

TIME FOR A RHYME   14

ache — break	cart — heart	motion — ocean	said — bread
bird — word	come — hum	plate — eight	shoe — blue
blood — bud	leak — shriek	power — flour	sieve — give
blues — bruise	light — height	rain — sane	thrown — stone
bore — roar	made — laid	rough — puff	work — lurk

ODD ONE OUT   14

Of the four words in the following lines three rhyme and one is the 'odd one out'.

bone	own	**shone**	groan	power	**lower**	our	flour
course	horse	**worse**	force	site	**eight**	height	right
hair	care	pear	**pier**	heard	bird	word	**sword**
toast	most	**cost**	roast	dear	**swear**	deer	mere
bowl	**howl**	soul	coal	**north**	worth	birth	earth
dumb	come	hum	**home**	weak	freak	meek	**break**
mown	loan	**clown**	lone	knew	new	**now**	due
no	grow	mow	**now**	**come**	home	comb	foam
raw	pour	**pure**	saw	**town**	alone	shown	flown

WASHY-WASHY ARGY-BARGY OR SUPER-DUPER RAZZMATAZZ?   15

airy-fairy – vague, impractical, unrealistic
bric-a-brac – small objects of little value
chock-a-block – full of cars, people or things
creepy-crawlies – insects
fiddle-faddle – waste time in a muddled way
helter-skelter – hurried and disorganised
hocus-pocus – confusing and deceiving
hodge-podge – a disorganised mixture
hurly-burly – noise and activity

mumbo-jumbo – meaningless ritual, nonsense
nitty-gritty – basic and important details
namby-pamby – feeble, sentimental, weak
palsy-walsy – very friendly with each other
roly-poly – pleasantly round and fat
razzle-dazzle – noisy and showy
super-duper – very good
teeny-weeny – very small
wishy-washy – indecisive, vague, half-hearted

STAR CHARACTERS 16

Here are some of the adjectives used in the horoscopes

active • arrogant • charming • critical • family-minded • friendly • funny • generous • hard-working • honest • impractical • kind • loyal • moody • optimistic • pedantic • penny-pinching • popular • quiet • reliable • romantic • selfish • sensitive • serious • slow • stubborn • unreliable • warm-hearted

Here are some of the phrases used in the horoscopes

always on the move • don't like conflict • don't listen to others • don't often show their feelings • easily make friends • full of energy • full of great plans • get bored quickly • hate being alone • hate rules • have a great sense of humour • have a high opinion of oneselves • have a lively brain • have a strong will • have no patience • have strong wills and personalities • learn quickly • like to feel safe • like to have power and tell other people what to do • lose touch with reality • love fun, jokes, parties • love practical work • open to new ideas • slow to change • take it easy • think that they always know best • try to hide their shyness • try to please everybody

COMPOSE A COMPOUND 18

Pair up the items below to form compounds.

SOLID COMPOUNDS	OPEN COMPOUNDS
milkshake	master plan
sunshine	oil tanker
raindrop	opinion poll
paperweight	package holiday
earthworm	picture book
handlebar	spark plug
strawberry	lunch hour
railway	safety pin
seatbelt	tennis match
sweatshirt	birth rate
songbird	police station
toothbrush	speed limit
guideline	sports car
letterbox	soup kitchen
tablecloth	pop star
snow plough	pot plant
mastermind	number plate

WORD PYRAMIDS 19

Add a letter to the previous word

1	l	p	a	e
2	it	pa	at	we
3	fit	pea	eat	wet
4	fist	pear	heat	west
5	first	pearl	wheat	waste

1	a	b	A	
2	at	be	an	
3	ate	bet	ran	
4	tear	best	rain	
5	crate	beast	train	
6	create	breast	strain	

SYNONYMS 20

Find the twelve pairs of synonyms in the verb list.

1. admire – **respect**
2. aid – **help**
3. alter – **change**
4. answer – **respond**
5. beat – **defeat**
6. begin – **start**
7. build – **construct**
8. cease – **finish**
9. comprehend – **understand**
10. deceive – **swindle**
11. detect – **find out**
12. scream – **shout**

Synonym Quartets 20

Pair up the synonyms in the grey box with their partners.

1. slow, sluggish, inactive, **dull**
2. affluent, rich, prosperous, **wealthy**
3. vain, arrogant, conceited, **proud**
4. afraid, fearful, worried, **frightened**
5. energetic, active, busy, **lively**
6. alien, exotic, foreign, **strange**
7. candid, open, honest, **frank**
8. tricky, deceitful, lying, **dishonest**
9. dark, dim, shadowy, **gloomy**
10. bad, immoral, corrupt, **evil**
11. lovely, pretty, handsome, **beautiful**
12. brave, courageous, fearless, **daring**
13. right, appropriate, fitting, **correct**
14. calm, cool, peaceful, **gentle**
15. glad, cheerful, content, **happy**
16. smart, intelligent, brainy, **clever**

Hair-raising Synonyms 21

For each adjective on the left there is a compound synonym on the right. Pair them up correctly.

frightening, disturbing	—	**hair-raising**	wealthy, rich —	**well-heeled**
mean	—	**tight-fisted**	gentle, loving —	**kind-hearted**
stubborn, obstinate	—	**pig-headed**	considerate, receptive —	**open-minded**
excitable	—	**highly-strung**	unreasonable, bigoted —	**narrow-minded**
tolerant, even-tempered	—	**easy-going**	woolly, confused —	**muddle-headed**
conceited, vain, boastful	—	**big-headed**	insincere, hypocritical —	**two-faced**
unemotional, unfeeling	—	**cold-blooded**	stable, sensible —	**well-balanced**
cheerful, happy	—	**light-hearted**	stupid —	**slow-witted**
arrogant, presumptuous	—	**high-handed**	forgetful, inattentive —	**absent-minded**

Of Compounds 22

Form compounds that complete the sentences.

1. ... the **cost of living** in cities is just too high.
2. What a **stroke of luck**! I found that ...
3. ... Ray was in a terrible **state of mind**.
4. The eagle is the most majestic **bird of prey**.
5. Most identity cards contain the **date of birth**.
6. ... It's not the **end of the world**, you know.
7. ... this film star is the **talk of the town**.
8. ... is the most well-known **work of art**.
9. The Queen is the **head of state** of England ...
10. The **guest of honour** will be the Minister ...
11. ... the oncoming traffic had the **right of way**.
12. ... Sue had the **presence of mind** to drag ...
13. Many people admire the American **way of life**.
14. ... has a right to their own **point of view**.
15. To make money is the **name of the game** ...
16. ... must be guided by a strict **code of conduct**

Looking Good! 23

Write the definitions from the grey box next to the appropriate phrase.

look after	care for, be responsible for	look into	examine in detail, investigate
look ahead	make plans for the future	look on as	consider, think of as
look back on	remember	look out for	pay attention to
look for	search	look over	examine quickly
look forward to	expect in an optimistic mood	look up	find out something
look in on	pay a visit	look up to	respect, admire

1. The trouble with many young people is that they live for the moment and don't **look ahead**.
2. **Look out for** the new Spielberg film. It's really very good.
3. The committee is **looking into** the government's new tax proposals.
4. Where have you been? We've been **looking for** you all over the place.
5. We are all greatly **looking forward to** Peter's party on Saturday.
6. Our friends were passing through our town and decided to **look in on** us.
7. Our neighbours will be **looking after** our cat while we are on holiday.
8. I can never remember Tom's address. I always have to **look** it **up**.
9. My mother has many excellent qualities, she really is a person you can **look up to**.
10. We always **look back on** that stay with you with great pleasure.
11. We have always **look on** Freya **as** a very special friend.
12. The professor merely had to **look over** the essay to see that it was too short.

Homographs 24

note	The singer could not reach that high **note**. / Lisa wrote a **note** for her husband.
spring	We drank from a mountain **spring**. / Of all the seasons it is **spring** I like best.
tap	I heard a soft **tap** on the door and opened it. / The **tap** in the kitchen is leaking.
ring	I'll give you a **ring** at the office. / Mr Rockgiver bought a beautiful **ring** for his wife.
tank	This car has quite a large petrol **tank**. / The use of the **tank** in warfare dates back to World War I.
match	Have you got a **match** to light the candle? / Did you see that football **match** on TV?
row	A furious **row** started when Mr Smith came home. / They are building a **row** of new houses.
bark	Don't mind Jim. His **bark** is worse than his bite. / A tree's **bark** is home to thousands of insects.
rest	After a good **rest** we continued with our work. / I will remember this holiday for the **rest** of my life.
bar	Tex went straight to the **bar** and ordered a whisky. / Many children like a **bar** of chocolate between meals.
race	The athlete won the **race** and received a medal. / Discrimination on the grounds of **race** is illegal.
party	I don't think any **party** is able to solve today's problems. / Our neighbours had a noisy **party**.
lead	Liverpool **lead** by three goals to nil. / Cars with catalytic converters must use **lead**-free petrol.
live	Gary Crooner always sings **live** on television. / It is my dream to **live** in the South Sea one day.

HOMOPHONES 25

Find the two homophones in each line.

hair	here	**hare**	her		too	true	**tow**	**toe**
no	**know**	knew	now		**sale**	sole	**sail**	salt
moat	mate	**meet**	**meat**		raise	**rose**	**rows**	rouse
slow	**sleigh**	**slay**	sly		**threw**	throw	**through**	trough
moon	**moan**	**mown**	mean		same	**some**	**sum**	seem
mile	**male**	**mail**	mole		soul	sale	sold	**sole**
loan	line	lane	**lone**		**brake**	broke	**break**	brace
ride	rate	**rite**	**right**		**wade**	weight	**weighed**	wide

Fill in the blanks in each sentence with homophone pairs from the grey box.

1. I'd **write** to her, but I haven't got the **right** address.
2. As we came to the coast we could **see** the **sea**.
3. Looking **for** the way, **four** riders **rode** down the **road**.
4. I was so hungry that I **ate eight** pieces of pizza.
5. One whiskey is enough, **two** would be **too** much.
6. My **son** always goes to Spain; he loves the **sun**.
7. The wind **blew** away the clouds, we had a **blue** sky.
8. If you come over **here** you can **hear** the waterfall.

ANTONYMS 26

Two of the words in each line are antonyms.

soft	slow	**hard**	nice		remember	**criticise**	**praise**	invite
medium	**strong**	**weak**	tired		steal	read	**borrow**	**lend**
shy	quiet	poor	**bold**		arrive	stay	**leave**	begin
short	**tall**	great	huge		conclude	**win**	play	**lose**
narrow	**wide**	long	high		remember	**forget**	think	understand
crispy	hot	**soggy**	clean		beg	**ask**	**respond**	reject
bitter	**sweet**	crunchy	tough		**admire**	show	see	**detest**
quiet	dark	pretty	**noisy**		do	stay	**build**	**destroy**
small	**common**	**rare**	afraid		**start**	move	improve	**finish**
first	second	middle	**last**		keep	**sell**	**buy**	give

DOUBLE ANTONYMS 27

For each of the adjectives in fat print there are two opposites.

soft	*loud* music	*hard* surface		**dark**	*light* hair	*bright* stars
good	*evil* spirit	*bad* example		**natural**	*artificial* light	*synthetic* fibres
sad	*Merry* Christmas!	*Happy* Birthday!		**dull**	*sharp* knife	*interesting* story
unknown	*famous* film star	*notorious* criminal		**strong**	*weak* coffee	*feeble* mind
small	*tall* tree	*large* country		**false**	*true* friend	*correct* address
thin	*thick* coat	*fat* cheque		**hard**	*easy* task	*soft* wood

Making Headlines

Pair up the headlines below with the texts on the opposite page.

1. People in the pretty village of Saxby ...
2. A group of senior Members of Parliament ...
3. Andrew Marshal, 54, chairman of Byte Electronics...
4. ... dispute over a group of leading doctors' suggestion to ban ...
5. ... the discussions on a lasting agreement ...
6. This is the most comprehensive and important investigation ever, ...
7. The 35-year-old mother of three had come back from a holiday ...
8. The Prime Minister promised a new plan ...
9. ... The expectations for a fall in the number of unemployed people ...
10. ... walkabout. The monarch filled old age pensioners with delight ...

Pair up the headline words with the equivalent words or phrases from the texts.

ROW – conflict	DOC – doctor	AGGRO – aggressive behaviour
UFO – Unidentified Flying Object	BOOZE – alcohol	HOL(s) – holiday/s
RIDDLE – mystery	OP – operation	MUM – mother
MPs – Members of Parliament	CLASH – dispute	CAB – taxi
BACK – support	TALKS – discussions	PM – Prime Minister
DRIVE – campaign	HIT – suffered a setback	VOW – promise
AXE – remove	BLAST – explosion	CUT – reduce
BOSS – chairman	KEY – important	£ – the pound
QUIT – leave	PROBE – investigation	HOPES – expectations
WED – marry	LINK – show connection	JOBLESS – unemployed people
PA – personal assistant	KIDS – children	WOW – fill with delight
TOP – leading	TELLY – television	OAPs – old age pensioners

CONFUSABLES • Adjectives

LAST / LATEST	E. Buchan's **latest** book ... / ... the **latest** fashion. / During the **last** five years ...
BIG / LARGE / GREAT	...but he was a **great** man. / ... a **big** black umbrella / ... there is a **large/big** garden.
ILL / SICK	My mother has been seriously **ill** for weeks. / The other day someone was **sick** on the bus.
LUCKY / HAPPY	I was **happy** to hear ... / He was very **lucky**.
FOREIGN / STRANGE	Did you hear that **strange** noise? / Five million **foreign** visitors come to England every year.
HIGH / TALL	... to make herself look **tall**. / ... the **high** mountains ... / ... the **high** walls ... prison.
ALIVE / LIVING / LIVELY	His father is still **alive**. / ... a **lively** conversation / I have no **living** relatives left now.
SYMPATHETIC / FRIENDLY	Joan was very **sympathetic** and understanding. / People in Britain are so **friendly** ...
QUIET / QUITE	This is **quite** a large house. Isn't it too **quiet** here?
LITTLE / SHORT / SMALL	Mr Pintsize is a **short** man. / What a pity that this nice **little** house is too **small** for us.
BRIEFLY / SHORTLY	... had met **briefly** once before. / **Shortly** after the meal ... / ... I told her **briefly** ...
HUMAN / HUMANE	The **human** body ... / ...the **human** race. / ... treated their patients in a **humane** way.
SENSIBLE / SENSITIVE	... a **sensible** decision / ... he's so **sensitive** / ... a **sensible** man. / ... **sensitive** children.
ACTUAL / PRESENT / TOPICAL	... his **actual** words! / Something **topical** concerns events happening at the **present** time.
EVENTUALLY / POSSIBLY	We **eventually** came to a decision. / I ... may **possibly** meet him then.
COMIC / COMICAL	All clowns like wearing **comic** hats. / ... there is something slightly **comical** about him.
ECONOMIC / ECONOMICAL	... the present **economic** climate. / ... people have to be as **economical** as possible.
ELECTRIC / ELECTRICAL	... the **electric** fire / ...an **electrical** engineer. / An **electric** plug / ... **electrical** appliances

MADE IN AMERICA   32

The words on the left are American English, the words on the right British English. Pair them up correctly.

American		British		American		British
apartment	–	**flat**		can (for food)	–	**tin**
baggage	–	**luggage**		French fries	–	**chips**
candy	–	**sweets**		line	–	**queue**
cookie	–	**biscuit**		pants	–	**trousers**
elevator	–	**lift**		railroad	–	**railway**
fall	–	**autumn**		station wagon	–	**estate car**
freeway	–	**motorway**		trash	–	**rubbish**
sidewalk	–	**pavement**		truck	–	**lorry**
subway	–	**underground**		vacation	–	**holiday**
yard	–	**front garden**		zip code	–	**post code**

WHAT'S COOKING?   33

Use American English expressions to complete the sentences below.

1. It's time for me to **hit the road**.
2. I **made a bee-line for** the fridge . . .
3. . . . you are **barking up the wrong tree**.
4. Al . . . has just gone home to **face the music**.
5. You can't just **sit on the fence**.
6. Don't **get hot under the collar**. Calm down!
7. We must . . . start to **play hardball**.
8. . . . what they say, 'Don't get mad, **get even**.'
9. M. J. **knocks the socks off** those other singers.
10. You must **make up your mind** someday.
11. All the parties **jumped on the bandwagon**.
12. . . . you could **to get away with** such a lie?
13. . . . a nice cool beer exactly **fills the bill**.
14. . . . everything will be fine. Just **take it easy**.

NOW YOU'RE TALKING!

Choose the correct questions or replies from the grey box and insert them where appropriate.

ON THE TELEPHONE

a. Folkestone 54854
b. Hello. This is Sue. May I speak to Jim, please?
a. He's out, I'm afraid. Can I take a message?
b. No, thank you. I'll ring back later.
a. All right. Bye.
b. Bye.

ASKING PEOPLE OUT

a. Do you feel like going to the cinema this evening?
b. I'd like that very much. Thank you.
a. I'll pick you up about 7.30.
b. Fine. See you then.

ASKING PEOPLE TO REPEAT THINGS

a. I'm afraid I didn't quite hear what you said.
b. I said 'Can I give you a lift home?'
a. Are you sure it's not too much trouble?
b. No, it's on my way home. Come on, jump in!

WITH A FRIEND IN A CAFE

a. What can I get you to drink?
b. A cup of tea for me, please.
a. How do you like it?
b. Very little milk without sugar, please.
a. Do you fancy something to eat?
b. Yes, I think I'll have a piece of cheese cake.
a. Right, I'll bring it over to our table.

APOLOGISING

a. I'm afraid I've broken one of your mugs.
b. Oh, don't worry about that.
a. I'm ever so sorry. Won't you let me replace it?
b. . . . I wouldn't dream of letting you do that.

TALKING ABOUT THE WEATHER

a. It seems to be clearing up.
b. Yes, much better than yesterday, isn't it?
a. Apparently it's going to turn warmer.
b. Oh. That would make a change, wouldn't it?

IN A RESTAURANT

a. May I take your order, Sir?
b. Yes, I'll have soup of the day to start with.
a. And to follow?
b. I think I'll try the vegetable curry, please.
a. Any dessert?
b. Just black coffee, please.

ASKING THE WAY

a. Excuse me, please, I'm trying to find the Tower.
b. Turn right, across the bridge. You can't miss it.
a. Is it too far to walk?
b. No, it's only about five minutes' walk.
a. Thank you very much.
b. That's quite all right.

SAYING GOODBYE

a. I've just called in to say goodbye.
b. When are you leaving?
a. I'm flying home tomorrow morning.
b. Have a safe journey. Don't forget to write to us.
a. Thanks, come and see me if ever you're in Berlin.

THANKING FOR HOSPITALITY

a. I really must be going now.
b. So soon? Won't you have another drink?
a. That's very kind of you, but I mustn't be too late.
b. What a shame!
a. Thank you very much for a lovely evening.
b. I'm glad you enjoyed it. Hope you can come again.

SHOPPING

a. Can I help you?
b. I'd like a large tin of cat food, please.
a. I'm afraid we've only got the small size left.
b. How much is it, please?
a. Seventy pence.
b. All right. I'll have two, please.
a. Anything else?
b. No, thank you. That's all.

Mixed Bag Quiz

This man is TAKING a photograph.

. . . present at a tennis match? – An UMPIRE

An **umpire** makes sure that the tennis match is played fairly and according to the rules. An **examiner** marks and judges the quality of an exam or of a product. A **referee** is in charge of football, rugby, boxing, wrestling matches. A **judge** works in a court of law and makes decisions about how the law should be applied, but the word also has a general sense, e.g. She is a good judge of character.

Three babies born at the same time are TRIPLETS

Triplets are three children born at the same time to the same mother. A **triangle** is a flat shape with three straight sides and three angles. A **tripod** is a stand with three legs on which a camera can be supported. Your **triceps** is the muscle in the back part of your upper arm.

An American calls it an elevator; in Britain it is a LIFT

A **staircase** is a set of stairs inside a building. An **escalator** is a moving staircase. A **radiator** is a heater, usually connected by pipes to a central heating system.

What are lines on the face called? – WRINKLES

Wrinkles are the lines on the skin which come with age. **Creases** are irregular lines that appear on cloth, paper etc., when it has been crushed. A **fold** is a bend you make in a piece of paper or cloth when you put one part of it over another part to make it stay in place. A **pleat** is a designed fold in cloth, e.g. a pleated skirt.

This girl has a SPLITTING headache

If you turn your back on people, you IGNORE them

The most exciting part of a story is its CLIMAX

All the other words mean **top**, e.g. the **peak** or **summit** of a mountain; also used in **summit** meeting or summit talks. Your **crown** is the top part of your head.

...want to make your house bigger you EXTEND it.

You **extend** your house or **build an extension** to it. Prices **increase** or you can **increase** your family. You **inflate** a balloon or a bicycle tyre; children and flowers in the garden **grow**.

Where would you find a congregation, an aisle and an altar? – In a CHURCH

Which of these persons pays rent? – A TENANT

A **tenant** pays money to live in a house which does not belong to him or her. A **proprietor** is the **owner** of a business, e.g. a hotel or a shop. A **landlord** is someone who lets you live in a room in his house, or in a flat or house that he owns, in return for payment or rent.

A fisherman uses TACKLE

A surgeon uses surgical INSTRUMENTS

You talk of gardening, farming and military **equipment**; chemical, breathing, gymnastic and heating **apparatus**; sailing and fishing **tackle**; medical and electrical **appliances**; surgical, scientific and musical **instruments**; the plough and the hoe are **implements**; in the kitchen you need cooking **utensils**; a **tool** is any instrument or piece of equipment you hold in your hand to do a particular kind of work, e.g. spades, hammers and knives.

... sort of person would you call a shark? – A CROOK

When a train does not arrive in time, it's DELAYED.

If you **postpone** something, you arrange for it to take place at a later date than originally planned. If you send **belated** birthday greetings to someone they come later than they should have done. A **retarded** person is backward, usually mentally retarded.

The time between day and night called – DUSK

Dusk is the time just before night (opposite of dawn). **Dark** means the absence of light but also nightfall. **Obscurity** means darkness or very dim light. **Gloom** is a state of semi-darkness where there is still a little light. Darkness is the opposite of light.

. . . use to move leaves? – A RAKE

A **rake** is used to move dead leaves or weeds into a pile. In the garden you use a **fork** for digging. A **shovel** is a tool like a spade and you use it for moving earth, coal or snow. You can use a **scoop** for holding food such as flour, sugar or ice-cream.

. . . extraction, drilling and filling? – DENTISTS

Which of these words is least strong? – To DISLIKE

If you **loathe**, **hate** or **detest** someone, you dislike him or her very much.

The words hammer, screwdriver and electric drill all have something to do with TOOLS.

Look for Links 37

1. Bear is to animal as bush is to **plant**.
2. Eye is to see as nose is to **smell**.
3. Author is to book as painter is to **picture**.
4. Loud is to shout as quiet is to **whisper**.
5. Man is to talk as horse is to **neigh**.
6. Bee is to honey as cow is to **milk**.
7. Sheep is to lamb as dog is to **puppy**.
8. Summer is to winter as hot is to **cold**.
9. Thought is to think as caught is to **catch**.
10. Mouse is to mice as child is to **children**.
11. Often is to always as seldom is to **never**.
12. Gloves are to hands as socks are to **feet**.
13. Two is to hands as ten is to **toes**.
14. Swim is to water as fly is to **air**.
15. Up is to down as top is to **bottom**.
16. Ear is to hearing as mouth is to **taste**.

Look in the Right Place 38

1. astronomer — **observatory**
2. bell — **clock tower**
3. cashier — **bank**
4. check-out — **supermarket**
5. dentist — **surgery**
6. diplomat — **embassy**
7. fruit tree — **orchard**
8. grave — **cemetery**
9. mechanic — **garage**
10. newsreader — **T.V. studio**
11. painting — **gallery**
12. professor — **university**
13. reception — **hotel**
14. roller coaster — **fairground**
15. sports teacher — **gymnasium**
16. warden — **prison**

Landmarks 39

Reunite the famous international landmarks, countries and geographical features.

The Great Wall of China
The Baltic Sea
Lake Constance (Bodensee)
Golden Gate Bridge
The English Channel
The United States
The Sahara Desert
The Black Forest
The Grand Canyon
The Pacific Ocean

The Eiffel Tower
Buckingham Palace
Saudi Arabia
Galapagos Islands
The White House
The Republic of Ireland
New Zealand
The Channel Tunnel
The Great Lakes
The Gulf of Mexico

Know the Ins and Outs 40

Use the verbs in the grey box to complete the sentences with the correct phrasals. Watch the tenses.

1. The guests **checked in** at the hotel reception.
2. You promised to help. You can't **back out** now.
3. Okay, I'll join your team; you can **count** me **in**.
4. The prisoners who **broke out** of jail . . .
5. Why does John always have to **cut in** . . .?
6. Dad promised me ten pounds, if I **clear out** . . .
7. . . . I'm just **filling in** for a colleague on holiday.
8. Dave and Fay have **fallen out** with each other . .
9. Why don't you **drop in** when you're in the area?
10. I have to **watch out** for those hidden fats.
11. . . . in the afternoon the rain **set in**.
12. Mr T. will soon have **sorted out** all problems . . .
13. . . . the police immediately **stepped in**.
14. The man . . . **turned out** to be a police detective.
15. How is Peter **settling in** at his new school?
16. I am sorry, but we are **sold out**, . . .
17. . . . we had to **call in** a service man.
18. . . . a difficult task often **brings out** the best . . .

GET YOUR TEETH INTO COLLOQUIAL ENGLISH   41

Complete the sentences with the colloquial expressions from the grey box; make changes where necessary.

1. . . . or are you just **pulling my leg**?
2. Let's **call it a day**. We can finish tomorrow.
3. I saw my friend . . ., but I **turned a blind eye**.
4. . . . Everybody just tries to **pass the buck**.
5. We've **pulled out all the stops** this Christmas.
6. The star's . . . **gave** the . . . **the once-over** . . .
7. . . . We were all **laughing our heads off**.
8. I thought I might find E. . . ., but I **drew a blank**.
9. . . . after lunch I suddenly **perked up**.
10. . . . it took some time to **get the hang of it**.
11. Could you **stick around** till Susan comes back?
12. . . . we were really **living it up**.
13. Politicians **promise the earth** . . .
14. Let Pete **have a go at** mending the radio, . . .
15. . . . you should **take it easy** for a while.

JUST LIKE A BULL IN A CHINA SHOP   42

Sue and Sean get on like a house on fire   –   They like each other and get on extremely well.

Dave slept like a log last night!   –   He slept very deeply and continuously last night.

Jenny has taken to her computer like a duck to water   –   She is naturally good at working with the computer.

The girls treated Fay like dirt   –   The girls treated Fay unfairly and with no respect.

He felt like a fish out of water   –   He felt uncomfortable and out of place.

Carol went out like a light   –   She was so tired that she fell asleep immediately.

. . . like water off a duck's back   –   Her suggestions have no effect at all. John doesn't take any notice.

IDIOMS OF COMPARISON   43

Pair up the idioms in the grey box with the definitions; then use them to complete the sentences below.

A. If something spreads very quickly, it spreads **like wildfire**.
B. If something is certain to make someone very angry, it's **like a red rag to a bull**.
C. If someone is extremely clumsy, he or she is **like a bull in a china shop**.
D. If a piece of news comes unexpectedly, it comes **like a bolt from the blue**.
E. If something fits exactly, it fits **like a glove**.
F. Someone who forgets things easily has a memory **like a sieve**.
G. If you know something extremely well, you know it **like the back of your hand**.
H. If people are fighting or disagreeing violently, they fight **like cat and dog**.
I. If things are selling very well and quickly, they sell **like hot cakes**.
J. Something that's very conspicuous, and usually inappropriate, sticks out **like a sore thumb**.
K. If someone is very bad-tempered and irritable, he or she is **like a bear with a sore head**.
L. If you reprimand or criticise someone sharply or severely, you come down on them **like a ton of bricks**.

IDIOMS OF COMPARISON 43

Pair up the idioms in the grey box with the definitions; then use them to complete the sentences below.

1. It's a pity this sweatshirt is the wrong colour because it fits **like a glove**.
2. My Dad never remembers my Mum's birthday. He's got a memory **like a sieve**.
3. If my mother ever finds out that I lied, she will come down on me **like a ton of bricks**.
4. Please don't wear that hat to the party. You'll stick out **like a sore thumb**!
5. I was too late to do anything about it. The rumour spread **like wildfire**.
6. Why don't you cheer up? You've been **like a bear with a sore head** for the past two days!
7. This is the best invention since sliced bread! The games are selling **like hot cakes**!
8. Mentioning animal rights to my uncle is **like a red rag to a bull.** He's a butcher.
9. My younger sisters don't get on at all. They are always fighting **like cat and dog**.
10. Jack has been a London cabbie for years. He knows the city **like the back of his hand**.
11. Stop being so uncoordinated and careless! You're just **like a bull in a china shop**.
12. The news of his mother's sudden illness came **like a bolt from the blue**.

FIXED PHRASES 44

Pair up the nouns and adjectives correctly.

alcoholic drink	identical twins	sacred cow
big business	mobile home	slow motion
central heating	nervous breakdown	special delivery
false alarm	private property	standing order
foul play	public transport	yellow pages

Use the fixed phrases to complete the sentences below.

1. Important documents should always be sent by **special delivery.**
2. A **standing order** at your bank is the best way to pay your rent each month.
3. Please keep out. This garden is **private property.**
4. They are **identical twins** and sometimes you really can't tell them apart.
5. When the police found the body, they immediately suspected **foul play.**
6. It is fascinating to watch the movements of a tennis player in **slow motion** on TV.
7. In parts of America you cannot buy an **alcoholic drink** if you are under 21.
8. The fire-brigade arrived very quickly, but it had only been a **false alarm.**
9. Trains and buses are the most widespread means of **public transport.**
10. A **mobile home** is a large movable caravan which people live in permanently.
11. Everybody talks about wage restraint, but directors' salaries seem to be a **sacred cow.**
12. In some countries illegal drugs have become **big business.**
13. Where can I get this picture framed? – Why don't you look in the **yellow pages.**
14. **Central heating** is a good thing, but the air often gets very dry in the rooms.
15. We've had so much work at the office lately that the boss had a **nervous breakdown.**

Up or Down? 45

Write the explanations in the grey box next to the appropriate phrasal verbs.

raise, educate children — **bring up**
admire, respect — **look up to**
invent, create — **make up**
confuse — **mix up**
build, erect — **put up**
tolerate, accept — **put up with**
be quiet, stop talking — **shut up**

close down — shut, cease to operate
settle down — live a regular quiet life
bring down — reduce
pull down — demolish
let down — disappoint
pour down — rain very hard
turn down — refuse

Use the phrasal verbs to complete the sentences. Take care to choose the correct tense forms.

1. . . . **pulled down** his garage, . . . **put up** a . . .
2. . . . **looks up to** him, . . . he has **let** her **down** . .
3. It was **pouring down** all day, . . .
4. . . . has **brought down** the number of road deaths.
5. . . . a lot of shops had to **close down**.
6. . . . she **turned** him **down**.
7. I wish Tim would **shut up**; . . .
8. . . . she has **settled down** in a quiet village.
9. I'm not prepared to **put up with** R.'s behaviour.
10. Carla **brought up** her children to recognise . . .
11. This writer **makes up** good stories for children.
12. . . . people often **mix us up** .

All's Well That Ends Well 46

Choose from the words in the grey box to complete the words in each group.

black–	skate–	side–	**board**	buzz–	pass–	cross–	**word**	tea–	pepper–	flower–	**pot**
leg–	bath–	show–	**room**	sand–	news–	wall–	**paper**	house–	speed–	life–	**boat**
hand–	note–	cook–	**book**	street–	moon–	flood–	**light**	rail–	motor–	gang–	**way**
space–	gun–	cruise–	**ship**	pipe–	head–	hair–	**line**	fire–	back–	sea–	**side**
boat–	green–	light	**house**	river–	flower–	sun–	**bed**	team–	home–	house–	**work**

Ladies and Gentlemen! 47

Pair up the elements in the grey box, forming expressions that complete the sentences below.

1. I've been searching for you **high and low**.
2. Dad built this shelf from **bits and pieces** . . .
3. . . . it all went **nice and easy**.
4. I'm **sick and tired** of all this rap music . . .
5. **Drinking and driving** is one of the causes . . .
6. . . . we must get in the latest **facts and figures**.
7. . . . tough **law and order** politics . . .
8. . . . one of those **sun and fun** holidays.
9. My firm have strict **rules and regulations** . . .
10. . . . when I'm **dead and gone**.
11. . . . from my own **flesh and blood**.
12. I will just . . . enjoy the **peace and quiet**.
13. Elvis Presley is . . . the king of **rock and roll**.
14. . . . It may be a **life and death** situation.
15. I've been working . . . **day and night**.
16. Many tourists . . . prefer **bed and breakfast** . .

Add your Ad   48

Here are some of the typical expressions and phrases used in the advertisements.

Shark Reef
unique • teeming with man-eating sharks • amazing creatures • You won't believe your eyes • man-eating monsters of the deep • razor-sharp teeth into pieces of fish • inches away from our divers' bodies • Your friends won't believe you • you've got what it takes • come face to face • one of the most ferocious creatures on this planet • action-packed adventure • unforgettable experience • divers come from all over the world • strange undersea phenomenon • feel the thrill and the shudder • the most extraordinary dive of the century

Bavaria
views and values have changed little • Relax and breathe freely • the peace of our glorious landscape • gentle meadows • cows peacefully grazing • the majestic Alps • the romance of fairy-tale castles • baroque splendour • weave their magic on you and transport you to the timeless quality of peaceful country living • Friendly people offer you a warm welcome • Join the locals • merry oompah music in the market-place • Taste the traditional local specialities • something for every taste and every pocket • children are welcome

The Best Tomato Ever!
revolutionize • a breakthrough • if you act quickly, you can be one of the FIRST • Let others follow where you lead! • Incredibly Delicious Taste! • fabulous Tomato • the all-time champ • bursts forth with juicy goodness • mouthwatering flavour • an intense delicious taste • super-juicy fruit • a whopping 12 inches • you simply cannot possibly imagine • absolutely delicious • imagine the taste-thrills • amazingly delicious mega-Tomatoes • You'll be the hero of your family • the hit of your neighbourhood • these spectacular beauties • big blockbuster superstar beauties

The best of Everything
'High Quality' • 'The Best of Everything' • watchwords of success • world-famous house • the finest foods and wine • exclusive fashions and perfumes • luxurious gifts of quality • Pride in Service

Who is who?   50

1. A **couch potato** is someone who spends most of his time at home watching TV.
2. A **rough diamond** has outwardly unpolished behaviour, but is at heart a good person.
3. A **stick-in-the-mud** doesn't want to try anything new, but always keeps to old routines.
4. A **heart-throb** is a man (often a film or pop star) who is very attractive.
5. A **stuffed shirt** sticks to the rules in a formal, self-important and inflexible way.
6. A **snob** thinks that his tastes and manners are better than those of others.
7. A **bully** uses his strength or power to frighten or hurt others.
8. A **spendthrift** is a person who spends money in a wasteful and stupid way.
9. A **fusspot** is always complaining and very difficult to please.
10. A **wannabe** tries to be like a film or rock star by imitating them.
11. A **nosey-parker** wants to know things which are none of his business.
12. A **daredevil** enjoys doing dangerous things.
13. A **gatecrasher** comes to a party without having been invited.
14. A **night owl** habitually stays up late or likes to work at night.
15. A **whizz-kid** is highly successful very quickly because of his / her clever ideas.

GERUND COMPOUNDS 51

Make compounds by pairing up the elements in the grey box, then use them to complete the sentences.

1. Can you tell me the **dialling code** for the US?
2. The family are all sitting in the **living room**.
3. Tomorrow is the **opening night** . . .
4. . . . have excellent **playing fields**.
5. The slums are seen as a **breeding ground** . . .
6. . . . in the regatta in his new **sailing boat**.
7. . . . **chewing gum** is good for your teeth.
8. Get your **swimming costume**!
9. . . . you need a nice, warm **sleeping bag**.
10. You'll need a **boarding pass**, . . .
11. The biggest **stumbling block** for . . .
12. . . . the **running costs** are just too high.
13. His marriage was the great **turning point** . . .
14. His **eating habits** are disgusting!
15. The Riviera is the traditional **meeting place** . . .
16. Since my uncle got his **hearing aid** . . .

MORE AMERICAN & BRITISH ENGLISH 52

American English (AmE) and British English (BrE) sometimes have two different words for the same thing.

PAGE 52

| AmE | station wagon | AmE | bill | AmE | buffet |
| BrE | estate car | BrE | bank note | BrE | sideboard |

| AmE | adhesive tape | AmE | German shepherd | AmE | baby carriage |
| BrE | sticking plaster | BrE | Alsatian | BrE | pram (perambulator) |

PAGE 53

| AmE | pacifier | AmE | French fries | AmE | billfold |
| BrE | dummy | BrE | chips | BrE | wallet |

| AmE | faucet | AmE | shades | AmE | trailer |
| BrE | tap | BrE | sunglasses | BrE | caravan |

| AmE | street car | AmE | street musician | AmE | trash can |
| BrE | tram | BrE | busker | BrE | dustbin |

| AmE | truck | AmE | tic-tac-toe | AmE | cookies |
| BrE | lorry | BrE | noughts and crosses | BrE | biscuits |

CONFUSABLE NOUNS 54

The following nouns are often confused. Write the correct word in the sentences below.

1. My **wife** is a solicitor. She's the only **woman** . . .
2. There are many spelling **mistakes** in your essay.
3. Good **luck** with your maths test!
4. We didn't buy that car. The **price** was too high.
5. The football **match** yesterday was exciting . . .
6. How is **business**? . . . customers in the **shop**.
7. She wears a gold **watch** on her wrist.
8. Who was that **man** . . . ? Was it her **husband**?
9. We tried our **luck** at the gambling casino.
10. The law . . . is not the same for men and **women**.
11. The second **prize** is a trip for two to Florida.
12. Despite all her **faults** she's a nice girl.
13. Excuse me, is this the **men's** department?
14. It's not my **fault**; . . . you made the **mistake**.
15. My wife's **happiness** is my only concern . . .
16. The **clock** tower of the Houses of Parliament . . .
17. Has the **price** of eggs gone up again?
18. . . . there are many **shops** in the High Street.
19. I wish you and your wife every **happiness** . . .
20. Outdoor **games** are high on the agenda . . .

CONFUSING Nouns 55

Choose the correct word, then write a sentence containing the alternative word . . . / Suggestions and definitions

1. My daughter has got a summer **job** as a guide .... / He was out of **work** for seven months.
   Job: the work that a person does regularly in order to earn money
   Work: people who have work have a job which they are paid to do

2. Turn right and the second **building** on your left... / They have a **house** in Spain.
   Building: a building is a structure with a roof and walls, e.g. a house, a hotel or a factory
   House: a building in which people live, usually the people belonging to the same family

3. Amsterdam is a city famous for its **canals**. / **Channels** of communication; the English **Channel**
   Canal: a natural or artificial stretch of water for navigation or for draining or irrigating land
   Channel: a route that is used by boats to cross a particular area of water; often used figuratively

4. I'd love to bake a cake but I can't find the **recipe**. / Please ask for a **receipt** when you buy the books.
   Recipe: a list of ingredients and a set of instructions telling you how to bake a cake or make a particular dish
   Receipt: a piece of paper you give to somebody to confirm that you have received money or goods from this person

5. Mrs T. wrote the message on the **back** of the envelope. / He fell off the chair and landed on his **backside**.
   Back: the part of an object that is at the opposite end of the front • **Backside:** the part of your body that you sit on

6. New York is one of the largest **cities** ... / Eastbourne is a pleasant seaside **town** in Southern England.
   City: cities are usually large and most British cities have a cathedral. Officially, a city has a charter which gives it certain privileges.
   Town: usually towns are smaller than cities.

7. A **suit** is a set of clothes ... / They have just bought a new three-piece **suite** for their living room.
   Suit: a set of clothes (a jacket and a matching pair of trousers for a man; a jacket and a matching skirt or pair of trousers for a woman)
   Suite: a set of matching furniture used in a living room or a bedroom

8. She heard the **sound** of footsteps... / Don't make such a terrific **noise** when you come home late at night.
   Sound: something that you hear • **Noise:** a sound someone or something makes, usually loud and unpleasant

9. He smokes five **packets** of cigarettes ... / The **package** from Sue contained a book and two cassettes.
   Packets: usually a box made of thin cardboard, or a bag, in which a quantity of items or of a substance is sold
   Package: a fairly small parcel; an object wrapped in paper or a cardboard box which you normally send by post

10. I'm no longer in the **habit** of getting up .... / My mother likes to stick to all the old English **customs**.
    Habit: something you do regularly, often without thinking why you do it
    Custom: something people do because it is tradition or considered the right thing to do

11. The **cost of living** in Britain... / Why is **life** so short?
    Cost of living: the average amount of money that food, housing, clothing etc. cost each person in a country over a period of time
    Life: the state of being alive or the quality which people have when they are not dead

12. There wasn't enough **room** for everybody to move freely. / There was just enough **space** for a bed.
    Room: enough empty space in a place for people to be able to move freely or do what they want
    Space: the amount of area in a place, building, cupboard etc. that is empty

13. My girlfriend had left a **note** ... / Did you see the **notice** in the shop window?
    Note: a short, usually informal letter or message
    Notice: a sign giving instructions or information and which is put up in a place where people can read it

14. She never did any **homework** so ... / The best thing about a holiday is that you don't have to do any **housework**.
    Homework: work that teachers give their pupils to do at home in the evening or at the weekend
    Housework: cooking, cleaning, washing, ironing, shopping; things that are done to look after a home

BE AS GOOD AS YOUR WORD

Choose the correct word to complete these sentences.

1. Have you **done** your homework?
2. It's difficult for me to find a **suitable** flat.
3. My son works **part-time** at McDonalds.
4. My tolerance has reached its **limits**.
5. He is a carpenter by **trade**.
6. This newspaper always has catchy **headlines**.
7. She **locked up** the documents in the safe.
8. The **scenery** in western England is beautiful.
9. All passengers **survived** the crash.
10. Let's have a **break** for lunch!
11. I like my men tall, **handsome** and rich!
12. Anne is very **like** her sister.
13. The bus leaves from the **stop** nearest the school.
14. Brian was very **sleepy** so he went to bed early.
15. He often goes on business **trips** to France.
16. I can **assure** you I was there!

THE GOLDEN MIDDLE

Choose from the words in the grey box and combine them with the words in each line.

glass	**house**	boat	sweat	**shirt**	sleeve
sand	**bank**	note	head	**master**	piece
spot	**light**	house	book	**shop**	keeper
language	**school**	friend	heat	**wave**	length
oil	**field**	mouse	flower	**bed**	room
paper	**work**	force	pay	**day**	dream
post	**code**	word	school	**boy**	friend
super	**market**	place	gold	**fish**	monger

PROFESSIONAL COMPOUNDS

Pair up the words that belong together to get compounds expressing jobs and occupations.

1. tour **guide**
2. airline **pilot**
3. ballet **dancer**
4. car **mechanic**
5. computer **programmer**
6. construction **worker**
7. customs **officer**
8. newspaper **editor**
9. film **star**
10. traffic **warden**
11. football **player**
12. hair **stylist**
13. maths **teacher**
14. fashion **designer**
15. research **scientist**
16. security **guard**
17. sheep **farmer**
18. taxi **driver**

WHEN ALL IS SAID AND DONE — 59

PAIR UP THE EXPRESSIONS

In all – **in total number**
At all – **in any way**
For all – **in spite of**
All for – **in favour of**
All over – **finished**
All along – **from the start**
All round – **in all respects**
All yours – **you may have it**
All the time – **continually**
All the same – **nevertheless**
All of a sudden – **suddenly**
All in all – **in summary**
All over the place – **everywhere**

COMPLETE THE SENTENCES

1. He said **all along** that we couldn't afford it.
2. If you need any help **at all** . . .
3. I'm **all for** anything that makes life easier!
4. **For all** her money she's not a happy woman.
5. The wedding was **all over** when we arrived . . .
6. . . . There you are, it's **all yours**.
7. . . . she continued **all the same**!
8. **All of a sudden** there was a tremendous crash.
9. When we were in Cornwall it rained **all the time**.
10. . . . shoes and clothes **all over the place**.
11. **In all** there were seventeen cars lined up . . .
12. **All in all** we had a good day . . .
13. A very good performance **all round** . . .

A BUNCH OF QUANTITIES — 60

a **loaf** .... of bread
a **bar** .... of chocolate
a **roll** .... of toilet paper
a **packet** .... of cigarettes
a **bunch** ..... of flowers

a **bottle** ...... of wine
a **carton** ..... of milk
a **pair** .... of shoes
a **jar** .... of honey
a **tin** .... of cat food

1. . . . I didn't get a **wink** of sleep last night.
2. . . . a fresh **sheet** of paper for the test.
3. Just one **lump** of sugar for me, thank you.
4. A sudden **gust** of wind blew off Mrs R.'s hat.
5. He felt a **drop** of rain on his hand . . .
6. . . . the smallest **speck** of dust on your rifle.
7. . . . a marvellous **spell** of warm weather recently.
8. . . . I'll just go outside for a **breath** of fresh air.
9. A **flash** of lightning . . . a **clap** of thunder.
10. . . . on that new **stretch** of motorway.
11. . . . such a large **sum** of money at home.
12. Would you like another **slice** of cake?
13. A small **puff** of smoke came from the pipe.
14. A **lock** of hair fell over her forehead . . .
15. . . . a **glass** of water and a **bowl** of soup.

Scrabble 61

[U₂] [R₁] [T₁] [G₂] [N₁] [M₂] [E₁] [A₁]

age	ant	arm	art	get	gnu	gum	gut	man	mar	mat	mug	net	nut
rag	rat	rug	tag	tar	tea	ten	tug	aunt	game	gear	gent	mane	
mean	meat	menu	name	neat	rage	rang	rant	rate	rent	tame	tear	tent	
tram	true	argue	gaunt	grate	great	manure							

All Letters: ARGUMENT

[A₁] [C₃] [I₁] [S₁] [T₁] [D₂] [E₁] [N₁]

ace	act	ant	cad	can	cat	den	din	eat	end	ice	net	net	sin
tan	tea	ten	tic	cant	cast	cent	dead	dent	dice	dine	disc	neat	nest
nice	sand	send	tend	tide	dance	enact	scant	scent	snide	staid	stance	seance	

All Letters: DISTANCE

[R₁] [G₂] [E₁] [T₁] [R₁] [S₁] [A₁] [N₁]

are	art	ear	get	net	ran	rat	set	sat	tan	tar	ten	gate
gear	gnat	near	neat	nest	rage	rang	rant	rare	rate	rear	rest	sage	seat
star	tarn	tear	tern	anger	grant	grate	great	greet	range	stage	stare	stern	
astern	strange												

All Letters: STRANGER

Fixed Phrases 62

1. **First**	○ **aid**	○ **class**	○ **language**	✘ minister

First aid is the simple and immediate treatment in an accident or another emergency.
First class means excellent, of the finest quality, the best and most expensive type of travel or service, e.g. first class ticket, first class letter.
Your **first language** is the language you grow up with and speak best, your mother tongue.

2. **Double**	○ **agent**	○ **chin**	✘ milk	○ **standard**

A **double agent** is a spy who works for one country, but also for that country's enemies. • A **double chin** is a fat chin that makes people look as if they had two chins. • A **double standard** allows some people more freedom than others, although they should all follow the same rules.

3. **Fast**	○ **food**	○ **track**	✘ boat	○ **breeder**

Fast food is simple food like hamburgers, served immediately after you ordered it. • The **fast track** is the quickest and (seemingly) least complicated way of achieving a particular goal in life. • A **fast breeder** is a type of nuclear reactor. Finally, fast boats, as well as fast cars and fast planes, do exist, of course but the fixed phrase for this is **speed boat**.

4. **General**	○ **knowledge**	○ **election**	○ **strike**	✘ building

General knowledge is non-specialised knowledge, which everyone has or should have. • In a **general election** the electorate (i.e. all people who have the vote) of a country vote for the parties and people who are to represent them in parliament. • A **general strike** is a strike in which not just one professional group, but most of a country's workers go on strike.

5. **Free**	○ **enterprise**	○ **kick**	○ **will**	✘ air

Free enterprise is an economic system allowing people and businesses to compete without too much state control. • A **free kick** in football allows one team to kick the ball without interference by a member of the opposing team. • If you do something out of your own **free will**, you do it because it is your own decision and not because somebody else wants it or forced you to do it.

| 6. Green | ✘ ocean | ○ salad | ○ belt | ○ party |

A **green salad** is a simple salad made with lettuces and other green vegetables. • The **green belt** of a town is an area of parks, woods or fields which is protected by laws and cannot be built on. • The **green party** is a political party concerned with the environment.

| 7. Foreign | ✘ sun | ○ language | ○ policy | ○ body |

A **foreign language** is a language other than your first language, which you have to learn with a special effort. • **Foreign policy** is a country's policy towards other nations; the person responsible for it is a country's foreign minister, (Foreign Secretary in Britain; Secretary of State in the US). • A **foreign body**, e.g. a foreign body in your eye, is an object that is present in something else by accident and should not be there.

| 8. Personal | ○ assistant | ✘ dog | ○ computer | ○ touch |

A **personal assistant** (PA) is a person who does all daily secretarial work for someone.
A **personal computer** (PC) can be used independently by one individual.
The **personal touch** is the word for the special personal attention you give to a job or a person.

| 9. Golden | ○ handshake | ✘ darling | ○ age | ○ rule |

A **golden handshake** is a large sum of money an employee receives as a reward (or because it's in his or her contract) on leaving a firm (mostly used in Britain). • A **golden age** is time in which outstanding successes in a particular field were reached and everything went very well, e.g. the golden age of ocean liners. • A **golden rule** is an important strategy or rule to always remember in whatever you do, e.g. *My golden rule is to never buy anything on credit.*

| 10. Hot | ○ line | ○ dog | ○ air | ✘ heating |

A **hot dog** is a long sausage in a bread roll. • A **hot line** is a special telephone line on which you can receive information on particular subjects, e.g. the hot line of a computer firm for its customers or a police hot line; a special direct telephone line between heads of government is also known as a **hot line**. • **Hot air** is talk that is designed to impress, but has no real meaning, consequence or value.

| 11. Human | ○ rights | ✘ country | ○ being | ○ nature |

Human rights are basic rights that all human beings have.
A **human being**, a woman, man or child, is a member of the species homo sapiens.
Human nature is the basic way in which human beings behave and feel.

| 12. National | ✘ money | ○ service | ○ park | ○ anthem |

National service is a service young people have to do by law in their country's armed forces.
A **national park** is an area of land that is protected by law because of its animals, plants or scenery.
A country's **national anthem** is a country's official song.

| 13. Open | ○ secret | ○ question | ○ letter | ✘ mouth |

We speak of an **open secret** if something (that is supposed to be a secret) is already widely known. • An **open question** is a problem which has not been resolved, because people still have conflicting views on it. • An **open letter** is addressed to a particular person or institution, but is meant for a much wider readership and therefore mostly published in a newspaper or magazine.

| 14. Private | ○ detective | ○ property | ○ school | ✘ tree |

A **private detective** is not a member of the police force and can be hired for various kinds of investigations. • **Private property** is for the use of its owner only and excludes everybody else. • A **private school** is not financed by the state and you have to pay a fee to go there.

| 15. Public | ○ convenience | ○ school | ✘ taxes | ○ relations |

A **public convenience** is a toilet in a public place that everyone can use (British English). • In Britain a **public school** is a – quite often prestigious and expensive – private school. In most of the rest of the world it is a school financed by state authorities and providing free education. • **Public relations** (PR) tries to establish a positive view of a firm's or an organisation's products or doings in public opinion.

DIAL A WORD 63

Here are some examples of possible words:

3 Letters

age	are	den	doe	due
end	one	ore	red	roe	rue
sea	see	sue		

4 Letters

dane	dare	dead	deed	dose
dune	gene	goes	gone	gore
nose	rage	read	rear	rend
rode	rose	ruse	sage	sane
send	sore	sure	urge	

5 Letters

adore	anger	douse	error	goose
gouge	grade	noose	nudge	order
range	rogue	rouse	sedge	snare
snore	surge	under		

6 Letters

arouse	assure	dagger	danger	gander
garden	gender	grease	grouse	grudge
grunge	ranger	render	rugged	

More

asunder	degrade	erroneous	generous
onerous	resound		

All Letters: DANGEROUS

3 Letters

aim	ale	ate	bat	eat
mat	tab	tea		

4 Letters

able	bail	bait	bale	ball
beam	beat	lame	late	mail
maim	male	mate	meal	meat	tail
tale	tame	team		

5 Letters

bleat	label	table

6 Letters

babble	mallet	tablet

More

eatable	malleable

All Letters: TIMETABLE

TIPS  OR TEACHERS

HOW TO USE THIS KEY

The nature of the 'answers' in this Key will obviously vary according to the scope of the exercises and tasks; quite often they are just that: unequivocally correct and conclusive answers and solutions to the tasks presented. In many other cases, however, they merely represent an example and suggestion and may well be supplemented by additional and better alternatives. The word lists suggested for the word games, finally, are by no means conclusive and merely serve as a first catalyst. In this respect, the suggestions in this Key will ideally serve not as an end point winding up the language activity but become stepping stones for further work and discussion.

Identifying and finding the correct answers – though obviously an important initial stage – is only one step in the vocabulary expansion process; to make the most of the exercises it is important that not only the lexical meaning of each correct answer in a pairing-up or multiple choice exercise or word game is understood and explained by the students, ideally it should also be transferred into the context of a meaningful sentence or even a wider discussion of the lexical items or lexical fields.

In writing down the answers or crossing out words in pairing-up exercises it is advisable to first use a pencil, allowing for a non-messy way of correcting errors and mistakes.

PLAYING THE GAME

Word games are an extremely effective way of motivating students in a classroom, . . . although they may seem to be fun – rather than serious – activities, there is often a higher level of concentration and actual learning taking place than in many more conventional classroom exercises.
     Deirdre Howard-Williams, 'Word Games for Beginners'

The Increase Your Wordpower series tries to let teachers – and learners using the book for self-study purposes – make use to the fullest possible extent of the possibilities inherent in word games, quizzes and competitions. Properly presented and employed they can serve as a basis for a well-structured progress in vocabulary extension, both for presenting new language and bringing passive vocabulary to the surface within a new context. Also, they involve the students not just academically, but also emotionally and socially – making the results and the language learned in the process both more enjoyable and more memorable for that. The argument for the use of word games has been beautifully summed up by Deirdre Howard-Williams:

- Word games have something in common with all other games. Whatever the game there is always a clear goal to strive for – the goal of winning. As in sports, you can play singles, doubles or in a team. In singles, each student plays alone to find the answers and complete the puzzle before everyone else. In doubles, when a pair compete together, the skills of co-operation are added to those of competition. Students will need to talk to each other to share ideas and come up with the right solution. In team games, when a small group work together and pool their resources, students will be in the position of 'teaching' one another and will be very motivated to remember so as not to let their team mates down.

All this corresponds to the real uses of language and illustrates the relevance of games to everything we do, not only in the classroom, but in the wider linguistic world beyond.

- The games can be tailor-made to test and practise what the student knows so even those learners with very little language can have the satisfaction of completing a puzzle or winning points for their team. This is particularly important for adult learners who need to feel – and see – that they are making progress.

- As games are self-contained and finite in scope, students do not need to feel lost in a sea of language but are given confidence by their ability to carry out a specific task with a clearly defined end.

Deirdre Howard-Williams, 'Word Games for Beginners'

An important aspect of the use of Word Games in the classroom is to keep up or regain the momentum, once your students have exhausted the initial spurt of writing down the obvious and easy words and the flow of items gets sluggish.

One way of overcoming this impasse is to encourage students to find more words by replacing letters of words they have already found (tell-bell-sell; bake-lake-take) or make longer words by adding letters to shorter ones they have already found (<u>able</u>, <u>table</u>, <u>tablet</u>, st<u>able</u> / tar, star, start).

Another way of getting things going again is to give your students dictionary definitions of possible words that allow students to identify them and then find or produce them according to the rules of the word game afterwards.

Students do not have to confine themselves to drawing on the vocabulary they already know, but should be perfectly free to experiment with plausible-sounding formations, which they then check up with the help of a dictionary. In drawing blanks and striking gold in the process, they will not only enlarge their vocabulary in a motivated process of active inquiry, but will be using the dictionary in a meaningful and authentic way and gain competence.

Nor is the principle of 'Learning by laughing' to be underestimated. Students will almost inevitably come up with fantasy words, which can technically be put together with the letters; let them give 'Call-my-bluff'-style definitions of their creations – and let them exercise their imagination to the full. Let your students call their friends' bluff or let them discuss or embellish the definitions – not failing to eventually supply them with the linguistic facts, of course.